In the Beginning

Other Books by Rabbi Adin Steinsaltz
Published by Jason Aronson Inc.

The Thirteen Petalled Rose
The Strife of the Spirit
The Long Shorter Way
The Sustaining Utterance

In the Beginning
Discourses on Chasidic Thought

ADIN STEINSALTZ

Edited and translated
by
Yehuda Hanegbi

JASON ARONSON INC.
Northvale, New Jersey
London

Library of Congress Cataloging-in-Publication Data

Steinsaltz, Adin.
   In the beginning : discourses on Chasidic thought / by Adin
Steinsaltz.
     p. cm.
   ISBN 0-87668-514-9
   1. Hasidism. I. Title.
BM198.S795 1992
296.3–dc20   91-44061

Manufactured in the United States of America. Jason Aronson Inc. offers books and cassettes. For information and catalog write to Jason Aronson Inc., 230 Livingston Street, Northvale, New Jersey 07647.

My heart overflows with a goodly
theme; I address my verses to the king.
My tongue is the pen of a ready writer.

Psalm 45:1–2

Your search is well founded.

For Valerie Diker

A.S.

Contents

Contents

Translator's Preface

One of the oldest and most significant aspects of Jewish tradition is the ordering of creative thought as commentary on the huge accumulation of revelation and wisdom known as Torah. The greatest minds of every age – not unlike the many local sages who used to put their ideas and interpretations in writing – scarcely ever claimed to do more than offer to explain some text or custom in the tradition. No one had the impunity to be an authority, an original teacher, or even a serious critic. Indeed, the greatness of these contributors to a vast body of wisdom literature lies precisely in their humility. They did not aspire to originality; if anything, to "innovation" perhaps, or clarification. Thus it takes time to distinguish the creative thinkers from the simply genuine scholars in any one generation.

All of which is only to explain why, with all of his extraordinary brilliance and intellect, Rabbi Adin Steinsaltz prefers to provide us with no more than commentary. In fact, he is so intrinsically a part of Jewish tradition that he does not like to write at all; he would much rather talk, and talk to a small group of people eager for "Divrei Torah," which can be any form of genuine spiritual communication. He will not presume to say that he has a message; he will just engage us in discourse and let the light shine wherever it may.

It was I who presumed to put this book together. Out of the many provocative and profound ideas that quietly rose up and just as quietly receded into the oblivion of an ordinary listener's forgetfulness, I felt that at least a small part could be saved. After a painstaking selection of those talks that more or less concentrated on a particular conceptual pattern, the spoken word in Hebrew was translated into English, edited, and given literary form. The talks were based on textual material in *Torah Or* and *Mamre Admor Hazaken* by Rabbi Schneur Zalman of Liadi. The result is a rather unusual presentation which, in accordance with the Chasidic mode upon which it rests, swings from one topic to another with a deceptive ease—deceptive because there is always more than can be caught the first time. One is tossed from one query to another concerning the fall of man. And before one realizes that we are not on a quick trip through the Genesis story of the Tree of Knowledge, but grappling with some of the most profound aspects of human destiny, one finds oneself engaged in Kabbalah as a framework for dealing with these all-too-formidable problems of good and evil. A perceptive listener sighs with relief. There is a way to contend with the intractable paradoxes! One is not helpless.

Insight into the meaning of the Sefirot, especially Chesed (Love or Grace) and Gevurah (Strength or Fear), provides the tools. Then we are drawn into the contemplation of Gevurah as returning light – and this amazing discovery of man's capacity to give light back to God opens unexplored vistas of human potential.

Indeed, glimpses of new ways of thinking intermingle with long-held wisdom. And some of the traditional expressions of this wisdom in prayer and Torah study are brought forward to help us on the path to understanding. It can be an exhilarating inner adventure for those who are alert and open-minded. To be sure, it may also be rough going for those without any Jewish background – but surprisingly enough, it is possible. Rabbi Steinsaltz's lucidity makes it seem comprehensible even when one is only at the beginning. Light, it seems, has such a capacity. And, therefore too, I have desisted from adding explanations or notes. There are plenty of books nowadays to satisfy the intellectually and spiritually driven desire to know. To ignite this desire is perhaps one of the reasons for this book.

Yehuda Hanegbi

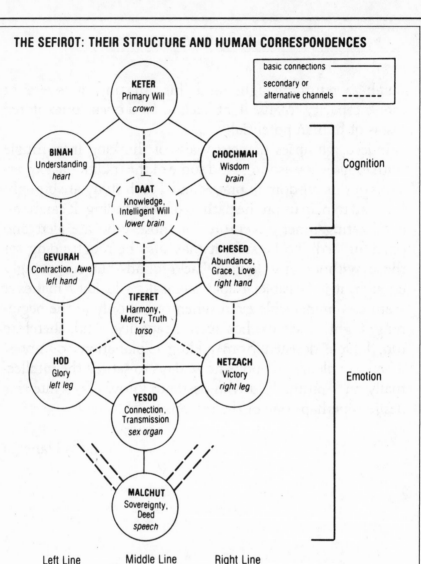

THE SEFIROT: THEIR STRUCTURE AND HUMAN CORRESPONDENCES

basic connections ————

secondary or
alternative channels - - - - - - -

KETER
Primary Will
crown

BINAH
Understanding
heart

CHOCHMAH
Wisdom
brain

DAAT
Knowledge,
Intelligent Will
lower brain

GEVURAH
Contraction, Awe
left hand

CHESED
Abundance,
Grace, Love
right hand

TIFERET
Harmony,
Mercy, Truth
torso

HOD
Glory
left leg

NETZACH
Victory
right leg

YESOD
Connection,
Transmission
sex organ

MALCHUT
Sovereignty,
Deed
speech

Cognition

Emotion

Left Line   Middle Line   Right Line

Malchut can be considered above as well as below the others, first as well as last. The broken lines from Malchut indicate that it connects itself with each of the Sefirot.

Daat and Keter are mutually exclusive; it is one or the other. Beyond cognition, Daat is superfluous; within cognition, Keter is not apprehendable. That is to say, Keter cannot be grasped with the mental faculties of cognition, while Daat is the necessary connection between intellect (cognition) and emotion (seven lower attributes).

This is only one version of the many possible diagrammatic representations of the Sefirot.

English translations of the names of the Sefirot: Keter–Crown; Chochmah–Wisdom; Binah–Understanding; Daat–Knowledge; Gevurah–Strength; Tiferet–Splendor; Netzach–Victory; Hod–Glory; Yesod–Foundation; Malchut–Kingdom.

Introduction

There are two kinds of secrets in the world, make-believe secrets and real secrets.

A make-believe secret is one that depends on its concealment; it is shrouded in mystery. Such a secret relies on darkness and the unknown. So long as it remains hidden, it arouses interest, but when it is revealed, the mystery vanishes and the secret loses its fascination. Such is the secret of the trickster and the charlatan, the stage magician and the mystigogue; their spell lies in the undisclosed, the mysterious wrapping. When the inner content or the trick becomes apparent, the magic disappears.

Such is not the case with a real secret. A real secret can be open and apparent to everyone. All can see the matter clearly and examine it from all sides. Nevertheless, the more it is looked at and examined, the more of a secret it becomes, profound and insoluble.

The story in the first part of the Book of Genesis is very well-known – children learn it at school, adults read about Adam in the Garden in many books – and still it remains a secret. And the more the extremely simple words of the Bible text are studied, the more numerous the aspects of riddle and mystery. Thousands of interpretations have already been written on Genesis, all trying to explain, reveal, and decipher the story – and still the secret remains inviolable, because the secret of the Torah is a real secret. As greater illumination is turned on it, new facets of inscrutability become apparent.

Consequently, additional contemplation or study of the story in Genesis does not propose to reveal the mystery of the secret or to make it more simple and comprehensible, but rather to disclose it further, to reveal additional sides to it. Every deepening of inquiry merely shows how these short, plain sentences lead to another intersection from which innumerable paths branch out, paths which a person can continue to trod all the days of his life.

In the Beginning

I

TOHU AND TIKUN

1

The World of Tohu and the World of Tikun

Among the first words of the Bible (Genesis 1:2) we have: "And the earth was without form and void." The Hebrew expression "Tohu" (without form) has a more extensive meaning in the writings of the Kabbalah, where it denotes the World of chaos or original substance and energy that preceded Genesis. It was only with the collapse of this World of Tohu that our world, the World of Tikun (Restitution), could come into existence. But the confrontation between the primal disorder and the amended order continues as a fundamental feature of reality.

The World of Tohu is also known as the realm of the broken vessels, from where evil comes. In this world preceding our own world, everything is jumbled together in its primeval state, and the parts are unable to combine or even to ease the friction between them.

The "kings" (see Genesis 36:31–39) of this World of Tohu fall and break because they are too complete in themselves; they are unable to unite or make real contact with anything outside themselves. They are unyielding and unstable. There are too many Lights ("Orot") and too few Vessels ("Kelim"). In the World of Tikun, however, there are fewer Lights and more Vessels. Thus, in the World of Tohu the Vessels shatter from an excess of Light which they are unable to contain. As in our own domain of ordinary things, when too much is poured into a "container" of any kind, it is liable to crack. When an idea has not the words to express it, we stutter. When anything exceeds its vehicle, there is danger of explosion.

Thus in the World of Tohu, the Divine Sefirot (Vessels or Kelim) not only cannot relate one to another, they cannot even support themselves. The Lights must remove themselves from the Vessels and they become the encompassing aspect of reality. Since the encompassing light cannot find its expression within the Vessels of reality, it has to remain beyond it. Without an appropriate vessel to connect it, the Light cannot be expressed in any inner expression. It exists only as an influence that has no particular channel of expression.

The catastrophe of the Vessels breaking and falling also influenced the Lights, which, unable to penetrate the Vessels, had to remain outside. The broken Vessels became fragments and fell into the lower world. But these same Vessels also belong to a higher world. Although insufficient to hold the vastness and intensity of the Divine Light, the shattered fragments are sufficient to constitute the raw material for a lower world. Indeed what we know as our universe is really the remnants of the broken Vessels of the World of Tohu (the Primordial Chaos). It is these fragments that constitute the World of Tikun, a shattered world that has to be corrected or reconstituted. Each fragment has its own force and individuality, but it no longer serves its original purpose; it is a broken vessel in every sense of the term. The fragments have become meaningless pieces of substance, of a quality that is destined to become weeds and stumbling blocks.

When a person experiences such a "fall," his light too is shattered, and what remains is a distorted self. He has to try to put together what was broken, for he is now in the World of Tikun and his task is restitution. Esau, the unfortunate brother of Jacob, became "wicked" as a result of such a falling. He was originally of a higher essence and was referred to as the bigger or older brother. And this too precisely because he came from the World of Tohu, which indicates that the primary root of evil in Tohu is higher than the root of goodness in Tikun.

To be sure, the matter is far more complex than any simple chart of higher and lower. For the world of Tohu is vast beyond comprehension, and correspondingly powerful, so that even the smallest fragments of its broken Vessels have considerable residue of force. The secret of this enormous force is in the intrinsic quality of Tohu as one-dimensional singleness of pure being. The parts cannot combine or make any kind of merger or unity with other parts. The world of Tikun, however, is characterized by its capacity to make combinations of the most intricate and varied sort. Thus the remnants of the World of Tohu have a rather terrible definiteness about them, a monomania, an inability to be anything else. This is apparent in the way

7

inferior forms of life are relatively fixed and rigid in their patterns of behavior when compared to higher forms of life, and of course to man, who belongs to the World of Tikun. The fragments of Primordial Chaos are with us in a great variety of forms. The creatures of Tohu are each splendid in their singleness of function, while man, who is able to combine many factors and reach another kind of wholeness in Tikun, can never be as swift as the deer, strong as the lion, or light as the eagle.

Thus the problem of good and evil seems to become focused on the struggle against the residues of Tohu. For man meets up with evil in its multiple variations at every step of his life. And the good impulse, for all its being very decent and sweet, has not much chance against the demonic singleness of purpose of the evil impulse. Would that goodness had such force! All that the good impulse can bring to bear is a certain plasticity and ability to make combinations.

Nevertheless, the very inflexibility of the forces of Tohu and their lack of orientation make them vulnerable. They are like the madness that strikes a person; in spite of its enormous energy, the fit will tend to destroy itself.

The World of Tohu, then, is indeed powerful but it is brittle and easily shattered, whereas the World of Tikun is stable, able to build itself up and continue its existence in a variety of forms. Thus when Jacob, the personification of Tikun, goes forth to meet his brother Esau after many years, he believes that just as he has now become more mature and whole, so too may Esau have developed. In this case, Esau would have become the rightful heir, the firstborn. For the World of Tohu precedes the World of Tikun, and when it breaks, the World of Tikun that follows has to repair the damage, make restitution, and correct the mistakes. But if the World of Tohu could make restitution of itself, it would remain the firstborn and the rightful heir. Had Esau reached Tikun of himself, he would be higher than Jacob. Commentators have been confused about Jacob's humiliating behavior, sending envoys with gifts and the like. The explanation of some Sages is that Jacob did not know whether Esau had attained completeness and maturity of being in the World of Tohu, in which case he would be on a higher plane and worthy of honor.

An ancient tradition concerning the precedence of Tohu lists the "kings who ruled over Edom before there were kings in Israel" (Genesis 36:31). These kings of Edom (Edom is Esau) are lords of Tohu, which are superior realms, but, as Genesis 36:32–39 succinctly tells us, they ruled and died one after the other. Had Esau been able to make proper contact with his original light, their history would have been different. Jacob was aware of the prototype his brother represented, and he even saw the great light behind him, and in this sense he offered him love and respect. But it was the interiorization of this light that made the World of Tikun possible, and this is what Jacob accomplished. The World of Restitution and Tikun (unlike the World of Chaos and Tohu) made fulfillment obtainable.

It seems, then, that there are two types: the man of the field, the exterior person; and the one who sits in tents, the interior man: Esau and Jacob. When they are together in harmony, they raise the world to its completeness. When the encompassing light is in a state of wholeness, it can also illuminate inwardly. The World of Tikun endeavors to elicit the sources of its own power from the fragments of the World of Tohu, by drawing forth ever more and higher forces.

In Biblical imagery, it is as though Jacob realized that he had completed his Tikun in the "neutral" world of oxen, donkeys, and servants; he had his wealth, his twelve sons, his honorable place among men. He was now ready to receive another illumination, another kind of Tikun, from the depths of Tohu, of Chaos itself. He felt that Esau might be the means of bringing him to it. In Chasidic terms, what is being considered is the transition to the higher level of Tikun, beyond that of control and order, into the ecstatic.

That is to say, the work of restitution in Tikun comes into its own after the attainment of order and control over life (which take their own time); its completeness is drawn from the encompassing light and power of Tohu itself. But the Tikun has to proceed in a certain direction; it has to build a life structure and dwell in it. When the design has been somehow completed, the light of Tohu can enter. Otherwise the Vessel will not be strong enough to hold the light of holiness. This is the essence of the mythical image of the broken Vessels. Man has to be a sturdy and well-built Vessel to receive the wild power of sanctity.

This statement seems to contradict some of the Chasidic notions about the need for a crushed and contrite spirit. But as the Rabbi of Pshische said, "There is nothing more whole and complete than a broken heart." For true blessing cannot enter a damaged or unclean place. Its power is of another order, coming from the outer light of Tohu; it shatters the world of partial Tikun and only a higher and more whole order of Tikun can absorb its influence. The present human world is still at a lower level of Tikun, where things have to be done properly in order to fit in with its limited and defined structure.

Nevertheless, when the world of Tikun realizes its task and the Vessel is finished, it will be able to contain the power of the World of Tohu. Then a third situation will have been created, higher than either Tohu or Tikun, a world in which the infinite power of primordial Tohu will be within (controlled by) the perfection of the World of Tikun. This world is beyond the known and proscribed and substantial, a world in which men are no longer creatures of rigid and finite design but can begin to act as combinations of both the infinite and the finite in a single being.

Thus when Jacob went forth to meet his brother Esau with gifts, he was saying, "I have completed my part of the task of Tikun; now give me your part of the encompassing Light and the Tohu and together we shall bring fulfillment." He had done what had to be done within his domain. The Talmud says that a person should be a sage, a hero, and rich in order to receive the gift of prophecy, because the Vessel to contain it has to be whole and sturdy. Even then, a person has to be forever improving himself.

Jacob's messengers returned with the distressing news that Esau had not changed. He had remained in the same nether world and was far from the World of Tikun; there was no way of bringing him to restitution. In esoteric terms, the World of Tikun and the World of Tohu could not do anything about the reality of evil here below. In spite of all he himself had accomplished within, Jacob could not cope with the evil outside himself. The world could not yet be redeemed from its fallen state.

The persistent old question presents itself. Why is the good so limited in its potency? Why is it that when purity touches uncleanness, it becomes unclean? Why shouldn't the unclean rather become purified by the contact? Of course there are several aspects to the problem. One is that the unclean and evil and all that this world represents are not affected by the World of Tikun. The World of Tikun can function only within a very limited sphere. It has its frontiers. It has to be orderly, quiet, understandable, and so on. And only within these prescribed limits can it function at all; so that it also contains prohibitions. Beyond these limits is the realm of evil, where the World of Tikun cannot move or make contact. There is simply no way of being in touch with evil as evil. Only when evil begins to change, whether of itself or by some other influence, can a process of repentance, or Teshuvah, begin to take place, by which the evil is made to approach and become integrated into the World of Tikun. So long as evil remains locked within its own sphere of evil, there is no contact with the World of Tikun.

Consequently, Jacob and Esau have to part. And what does Jacob say to his brother Esau, who proved such a disappointment to him? He tells him that sometime at the end of days he will come to visit him. These words suggest that when the world gets to its utmost completeness, Jacob (Tikun) will be able to come to Mount Seir, where Esau dwells.

It is written that Esau had 400 men to do his bidding. These represent 400 severe judgments (Dinim) or demonic forces that are released when evil is free to act destructively. These forces of evil are essentially parasitic. They are unable to do anything of themselves; they live in a vacuum, in a distorted emptiness and are sustained by the nourishment they get from holiness. And that is the problem—that evil feeds on the good, becoming ever more powerful through this sacred nourishment. As it was said at the very beginning to Cain: "For sin lieth at the door. Unto thee shall be his desire and thou shalt rule over him" (Genesis 4:7). Sin not only crouches there waiting, it also loves you and desires you. Because man is its very source of life, sin is a parasite living off of the human.

Indeed, evil's parasitic lust for man is never satisfied. But it is only theoretically true that evil can swallow everything. Some things, when swallowed, begin to work from within and break the inner logic of the "swallower." This can be seen in history: marauding tribes conquer (swallow) a higher civilization and are in turn swallowed up, assimilated into it. It can happen to a person, to an idea. When evil seems to destroy and disfigure, a process begins that has its own dynamics, in which evil is unable to absorb its victim, and the opposite takes place. Thus when a great idea is gulped down with zest, it can work in unexpected ways and cause unanticipated changes. For instance, the Roman Empire's destruction or swallowing up of Jewish life and ideas eventually became connected with its downfall.

In the larger perspective then, evil cannot really win because it has no substance. The more it swallows, to

13

survive, the more is it liable to crack at some point. "For a man shall rule another to his own harm," as it is said (Ecclesiastes 8:9). There are two processes at work simultaneously—the demonic destructive one of evil and that of Tikun—but since the evil subsists on the nourishment it gets from the holy, its influence is limited and sooner or later it has to surrender.

We are reminded of the comic story of the proud and successful robber who sent his son to school to learn manners, but the son learned his manners so well that he could not be a robber any more. The process of civilization has its own logic of decency. As the evil swallows the good, it is eventually influenced by the good to its own destruction. In the meantime it undergoes distortion upon distortion. There is a kind of circuit, like the exchange of merchants' goods, enriching some, impoverishing others, benefiting as well as injuring, but on the whole keeping things going in a certain direction. In the end, of course, "death itself shall be swallowed forever and the Lord God will wipe away tears from all faces; and the disgrace of His people shall He take away from off all the earth" (Isaiah 25:8).

II

THE CREATION
OF MAN

2

Formed from the Dust

The creation of man in Genesis differs from the creation of other forms of life. As it is written: On the third day, God said, "Let the earth bring forth grass, the herb yielding seed and the fruit tree yielding fruit" (Genesis 1:11), on the fifth day the creatures of the sea and the fowl of the air were created, and on the sixth day God made the beasts of the earth after their kind. Only afterwards was man created in the image of God. Each of the forms of life was made whole, the plants, animals, birds, and insects coming forth alive and separate in their uniqueness. Only man was formed first as an object, from the dust of the ground, and in order for him to become a living creature, God had to breathe into him the breath of life.

Thus man was first formed as primordial matter, without life or soul. Unlike the other living things of the earth, he had to go through various stages in order to become Adam, the creature that speaks.

It would seem, therefore, that the body of man is of a lower order than that of the beasts, who were never an inert

19

substance but were created alive and whole. Some Sages have argued that man is so primordial that he preceded Genesis, being the most elemental and lowest of all that exists as well as the highest.

The question is raised: Why does man have to be created from the dust of the earth?

To answer this we should inquire more deeply into the nature of the difference between man and the rest of creation. Existence is traditionally divided into four basic forms: inert matter, plant life, animal life, and that which speaks. Without going into the obvious distinctions among these classifications, we may conclude that man contains in himself all of them; made of material substance, growing like a plant, moving like an animal, and communicating through language.

To be sure it is not the ability to utter words that distinguishes man, but the capacity for conceptualizing and for communicating those conceptions. As someone once remarked, for all of a parrot's garrulousness, it is quite incapable of saying, "I am hungry." Notwithstanding our increased recognition of the subtle and varied modes of communication between individuals in animal communities, we have not been able to observe anything like the human expression through language.

There is also the fact of the animal soul, the initial life-force common to all living creatures. This is not the same as the Divine spark in all things that gives them form and life and that never comes to consciousness. The animal soul is more akin to the plant vitality, in that it is fairly restricted to basic physical functioning. It is bound to the material and the vital, and operates within the limits of a specific organism. As it is expressed in the Bible: The blood is the soul.

There is a significant leap to the next stage – speech. The unity of body and animal soul is broken. Something new and different has been added – a capacity to transcend the limitations of the body. This capability is not the cleverness to make tools or to be a more efficient food gatherer, or even to use the hands or head to manipulate the world. It is something that may even be considered a hindrance to efficient functioning, since it can't be used for eating, making a show (to attract or ward off others) or fashioning a dwelling.

No matter how primitive a man is, or how harsh his physical environment, this factor that makes him human is present. This is not the Divine soul or any essence that makes a man feel superior; rather it is his humanity, the reason for considering him to have been made in the image of God. What does it consist of?

Indeed, it may be only theoretical to speak of the Divine soul of man. In practice, man is an inferior creature, quite dependent on the rest of existence. The grass can get along quite well without man, but man needs the grass to cultivate it and transform it into bread. Man is human because he has a task in life to relate to the world, to raise it up and give it meaning and purpose. Otherwise the universe is an endless repetition, a question without an answer, a movement without a goal. When man makes bread out of the grass, the bread rises up through man and "prays and studies Torah." That is, it is lifted up out of the earth; its hidden sparks of holiness are released and it becomes a part of a higher level of reality.

This then is why man had to be formed from the dust, the most inferior of substances. When we want to lift something heavy with a hoist or a pulley, we have to anchor our leverage firmly on the ground. When we build a wall for a house, we make sure of solid foundations. Similarly, the Divine soul of man had to be fastened to something firm and steady like the earth. From this base the plantlike growth force in man could take root and the rest of his animal powers could issue. For man is also the lever and the hoist of all of creation, the factor that can raise the essentially inert parts of the world. Only with man's interference can the rest of creation rise out of itself. But man has to begin from where he himself issued, the dust of the earth, the most primordial and amorphous form of matter.

Man is also called "that which speaks," "Medaber" (מדבר). The root of this Hebrew word has several meanings, one of which is "to lead." Man thus is not only the spokesman of the world, he is the one who leads, who directs the world. Another image is that man is the driving factor in an immobile reality; he can progress and instigate change.

Why did this speaking creature, who is above all others, have to clothe himself in a body of inert matter? The answer to this puzzle is hinted at if one notes that the four forms of existence correspond to the four letters of the Tetragrammaton. The Yod is Medaber, the first Heh is animal life, the Vav is plant life, and the last Heh is matter. The crown of the letter Yod is considered to represent the

Divine soul of man. It does not appear as a letter but as an almost hidden segment or sign. Nevertheless, this "kotz" or crown of the letter Yod (י) is higher than the Yod. What is more, it cannot combine directly with any of the letters, which have an identity of their own; it has to approach the entirety from the other end; it can attach itself only to the final Heh, which represents the most inert and formless substance.

A circle is thus formed; the end meets the beginning. Indeed, it would seem that the end and the beginning have something in common that is of the very essence of the whole. As is expressed in the Hebrew word "Tachlit" (תכלית), the concept of purpose requires the simultaneity of both the end and the beginning. The end of the matter is in the nature of the beginning. The original idea contains the result; the final result contains the initial notion.

As it is written: "In Wisdom did God form the earth and in Understanding He made the heavens" (Proverbs 3:19). Heaven and earth are often viewed respectively as parallel to the spiritual and the material aspects of life. And there are many levels, just as one speaks of up and down in space, so that there can be said to be higher or lower. Thus matter can be viewed as material, that is, of the earth, and the plant as spiritual, or of the heavens.

To proceed further, in Kabbalistic terms, the Attributes, or Sefirot, are associated with the plant (Tzomeach), characterized by many alterations and growths. Feeling or emotion is connected with the attributes and moves up and down; it has a dynamic aspect, able even to change and transform itself, to grow and move on to another level of

23

being. The letters (of the alphabet) correspond to inert matter (Domem), which does not experience organic growth. The "Word," therefore, is in itself static, being made up of letters. Indeed the inertness of letters is so marked that they are sometimes called stones, building stones that are used to construct a house but have no life of their own.

What seems odd is that in terms of the Attributes, Chochmah (Wisdom) is connected with matter and with words, while it is Binah (Understanding) that is connected with plant life and emotion. One would tend to see it the other way round, since Chochmah is pure consciousness, a passive receptor of the flash of light in terms of the idea, while Binah is the development of the idea or of the original apprehension. But feelings, it seems, cannot receive from Chochmah; they get what they require from Binah. It is the contemplation of a thing that creates emotion. And irrespective of how a feeling comes into being, its continued existence, sustenance, and growth depend on some sort of contemplation, mental or otherwise. A pure consciousness does not in itself have any emotional power. A subject has to be thought about, considered in some way; the imagination has to be involved, and a structure has to be formed in the mind that is expressed as emotion. It is over the process of contemplation that one has a degree of control, whereas the flash of Wisdom seems to overwhelm us. The ability to consider something enables one to form an emotional relation to it.

Chochmah is thus unable to create emotion, being too high, or in any event, above the contact. To be sure, there is far more to be said about the action of Chochmah and how

24

it relates to the secret of the word, or the letter, making speech the quality that characterizes man (Homo sapiens). Man is thus not the creature that feels, he is that which talks. It is the human capacity to create symbols that seems to be his highest achievement, even though signs and symbols may be considered abstract and lifeless ideational forms. In any case they are not full of movement and life, like feelings. Still, symbols do belong to a higher mode of consciousness, to the same power as speech. Infants certainly feel strongly, long before they can talk. That is, speech belongs to a higher category than emotion.

This brings us back to the other end of the circle. The body of man is not considered to belong to the order of Tzomeach (Plant) but to the order of Domem (Inert Matter), because of man's having been created from the earth, after which the breath of life was breathed into him and man received a Divine soul in the aspect of sublime Chochmah. As it is written "And by Wisdom was the earth created." That is to say, the earth, inert matter, was formed from something of the highest order, which is parallel to the paradox stating that it is the creation of matter that is the wonder of Genesis. Wondrous is the creation of matter and not the creation of spirit – matter, after all, is so very material and far from the spiritual factor that creates.

Whence the tremendous power of the word? After all, the power of the word lies not only in its being the subject or instrument of a concept, but in the fact that of itself it stimulates and brings forth the idea. Which is to say that words are like horses. A horse can't do much on his own, but when a man rides him he can go far. Words need riders.

Man thus was made of both dust and spirit, of inert

matter and of sublime wisdom. His body and soul are intrinsic components, making him "Medaber," the one who speaks. Unlike the Tzomeach (Plant) and Chai (Animal) orders, which are congruent, Medaber (Speaker) and Domem (Inert) are distant from one another. But their very oppositeness makes their meeting a closing of the circle which is man.

The name Elohim is related to nature, the elementary forms of creation, which we may call reality of the world. The Lord God (YHVA) is the Divine name beyond existence. But man cannot be created from this beyond; he has to be formed by the combination of form and purpose, the putting together of the end and the beginning. He is therefore made of the dust of the earth and the sublime spirit of God. His Divine soul is not even the same animal soul of creatures; he is a paradox of the lowest and highest.

The trouble seems to be that this human soul cannot speak directly to the celestial beings, it can only make contact with the lower orders of existence. As it is suggested in the Kabbalistic writings, Abba or Father (God) created the earth (Malchut) from the aspect of Chochmah (Wisdom), so that the end of the matter (Malchut) is bound up with the beginning, or the utmost (Keter), of the Tree of Life.

3

Direct Light and Returning Light

It is written: "And the Lord God said, It is not good that the man should be alone; I will make him a helpmate against him" (Genesis 2:18). What is most puzzling is the word "kenegdo," כנגדו, "against him." The emphasis seems to be on confrontation or opposition, and not (as the New English Bible puts it) to be his partner. But, of course, what is being discussed refers only to the celestial worlds and should not be taken as a directive for human conduct in this world.

There seems to be a deep concern for man behind the words, "It is not good for man to be alone," expressing that Divine aspect described in Psalms 84:12, "For the Lord God (YHVH Elohim) is a sun and shield." The name of God here is YHVA, which in Hebrew may be translated as "being," or that which brings into being.

However, the coming into being of all-that-is through the direct intervention of God would have left each and every thing unable to function as a separate entity. The Divine Light would be too dominant and no single essence could withstand it sufficiently. God Himself had to fashion some sort of shield to protect the world from His name (or direct encounter). Hence the statement: For the Lord God (YHVH Elohim) is a sun and a shield. That is, there is both a burning sun (YHVA) and a something to shield the world from the sun (Elohim). Elohim is the form of the Divine that protects creation from being consumed in the all absorbing light of God (YHVA) the Creator.

Elohim thus assumes the aspect of "Tzimzum" (Withdrawal or Contraction) as part of the attribute of Gevurah (Severity or Strength), restricting the Divine Light so that each created entity can feel its separate self and not become absorbed in and swept away by that Light.

The name Elohim has therefore become associated with many of the human experiences of the Divine, such as power, omniscience, holiness, or justice. In many ways it evokes the aspect of God as ruler, king, or judge. There is no king without a kingdom of subjects. And the subjects are not the same as the members of a family or a household (where love rules); there has to be a certain distance between ruler and subjects. Too much closeness or intimacy makes sovereignty impossible. The name Elohim represents this aspect of separation and concealment of the Divine.

The commandment or mitzvah to believe in God is not a mandatory order to have faith, because faith or belief in God is assumed to be self-evident, flowing from the essence of man. The commandment merely refers to complete recognition that Elohim also is God, that the hidden, the shield, too is Divine. The YHVH of all inclusive being contains Elohim, the aspect of God hidden behind the rule of Judge or

King and all the many levels of the same function of sun and shield.

Similarly, Shechinah is the Divine name for Malchut. Just as Elohim is the name for the ruler or king, Shechinah serves to represent the kingdom. Because Shechinah means the indwelling one, as it is written, "And I shall dwell among them," ושכנתי בתוכם (Exodus 25:8). That is, God lives in all created things. Otherwise created things could not know God at all; indeed it is only because the Divine dwells in them that they can react to stimuli. To be sure, God can accomplish this only if He remains incognito, unrecognized as it were. His light, were it manifest, would demolish the separate existence of things. In other words, God has to conceal himself in order to dwell in reality.

This concealment, which is a part of the Divine penetration into all created things, has resulted in the existence of beings who consider themselves to be separate individuals, as though the world had been formed and evolved so that they could assert their own personal existence. All of which is again intended to lead to the self-nullification of this separate being in an ultimate surrender to Divine Unity. Just as all the celestial beings give themselves up to God, so too is it meant that earthly creatures should similarly nullify themselves. For God made the world and independent existences in order to bring them to Him. "That which is" eliminates itself in favor of "that which is not." Glory is that which comes from this surrender, this yoke of the Kingdom of Heaven. But to realize this ultimate higher purpose, there has to be a consciousness of separate existence to begin with.

The Tzimtzum (Divine Withdrawal) does not work in

31

only one direction. The world is not an illusion, a "maya" or hallucinatory dream. It does have a real existence, but as a Divine shield, God as Elohim. The concealment manifests itself in the form of a reality, a reality that hides the Divine Light. To give another inadequate illustration: I can hide or disguise myself in a number of ways: by wearing different garments, by putting my hands in front of my face, by covering my eyes. Whether I conceal myself from myself or from others, I remain the same one. Thus YHVH Elohim is one, the sun and shield, the two names of Divinity. The aspect may be of one who gives forth light or of one who is in darkness, but the manifest one and the hidden one are the same one. Because the hiddenness is indeed real, creatures may feel separate and enjoy the freedom to determine their own essence and to do some things on their own.

It is like learning to play the piano. Both hands have to be taught, each one to play independently of the other. At the same time, they have to play in harmony, in absolute coordination. For one hand to play its own music would be disharmony, wrongness. In other words, the freedom allowed to man to determine his own essence is like the independence accorded to the hand to play its own music, even though without coordination there is no harmony, no rightness of execution. Our freedom to do as we choose is also the freedom to err, to get out of rhythm and to do the wrong thing.

This brings us to another explanation of the term "avodah zarah" (idolatry)—besides defining it as that which does not necessarily exclude the acceptance of a highest God over all; it also refers to that which simply insists on the absolute independence of a self that is not the one God. When someone sees himself as altogether independent of the absolute, he is in Galut, a state of being or place of spiritual banishment called Exile of the Shechinah.

After all, what is exile? It is obviously not another place, a location to which one may move willingly or not. Indeed most change of place is an act of consciously enjoying a variety of scene, a trip. Galut results from the will of others who decide where to go and what to do. It is not unlike captivity or subjugation, since there is no freedom to choose. One may jokingly say it is like the difference, for the driver of a vehicle, between being at work or on vacation. The freedom to go where one chooses is the essential, or at least the feeling of such liberty.

It may be maintained that God is everywhere, that it does not matter where one is or where one is going. And since there is no place without Shechinah, to be exiled from it has no meaning. In answer to which a certain illustration may be used. If the Shechinah is quite definitely present, at least there where a minyan of ten are gathered in prayer, then the Galut of the Shechinah occurs when someone of the minyan engages another in conversation during the prayer. The secret of the Galut of the Shechinah is in the rejection of the Divine Kingdom. Some know that God is King of the Universe and accept it; some either are not willing to accept it or do not know enough to make a decision on the matter. Whichever the reason, the Galut of the Shechinah results from any repudiation of the sovereignty of God at any time, in any place.

Thus the Shechinah is "exiled" during the course of every

human life. Not only when one sins, but even when one "compels" God (or the laws of life and nature) to do one's own will. By misusing things that exist in the world, one can make the Divine hide Himself and withdraw. All of which is a background for the essential point concerning the Divine duality of God as both sun and shield, as He who reveals Himself and He who conceals Himself!

The Shechinah, the indwelling One, is sometimes called a mirror. As it is written concerning Moses: "I the Lord make myself known to him in a vision (mirror)," במראה אליו אתודע (Numbers 12:6). It is called a mirror because it may be conceived as that which provides only a reflection of the thing, not the thing itself, that it even obstructs one's field of vision, whereas where there is something transparent, I can see through it and clearly discern what is beyond. Another aspect of the mirror is its capacity to show me things I may not be able to perceive otherwise, such as that which is behind me or out of my range of vision. Thus the mirror not only reflects what is known, but can provide something that does not otherwise exist for me. It seems to create another reality.

A mirror can do this because the glass is coated with silver that covers and hides the surface, preventing vision from penetrating. This obstruction causes the light to return, making vision reflect back, and gives me knowledge of something that is behind me. The coating provides an insight into something not ordinarily visible.

The glass itself is not the important factor. Any smooth, even surface, such as certain metals, will do. The quality of the mirror depends on the covering of the glass. If it is too heavy or thick, it is nothing but an obstruction. It has to be made of shiny material that lends itself to thin, even spreading. The light cannot be swallowed up; it has to be reflected back. Indeed, making mirrors is an art. Some mirrors, like those in telescopes, are almost perfect in their capacity to reflect a true image without distortion. The secret of the mirror lies in the care that one takes to make it what it should be.

We can consider the action of the Divine Light in the same way. The function of the aspect of Elohim is to cover and hide the basic substance and reflect back the original light. Its total effect is Tzimzum, a withdrawal effect.

The efficacy of the mirror lies in its retarding the light, not letting it spread further, and deflecting some of it. The returned or reflected light can do things that the original light cannot do. It can reveal what is behind me as well as what is before and around me. It manifests a new reality. It can be used to perform tasks otherwise impossible. It can go around corners as in a periscope, can create a global vision of 360 degrees, or can enhance the size of the visible a thousandfold and more as in the telescope. In other words, even though the mirror acts as a diminishing or even obstructing factor, deflecting and interfering with the flow of light, it is nevertheless a creative element, making it possible to experience new things, see new things.

What is more, the returning light can exceed the power of the direct light in certain ways. As it is written "the wife of valor is the crown of her husband" (Proverbs 12:4). The wife who receives, she who is properly receptive, achieves a level of being that not only is equal to that of her husband,

35

but goes further, to a higher level, which is the "glory" of the husband.

The power to reflect properly is thus also a power to create. And the returning light can even exceed the original light. Thus, for example, the lower altitudes of the earth are warmer because the light keeps getting reflected back upon itself. The rarer heights – where there would seem to be more light – are so much cooler that life itself is impossible. That is to say, we live on earth by virtue of the reflected light of the sun in the atmosphere, not by the power of direct sunlight.

Similarly the Sabbath day receives light and meaning from the days of the week but it reflects back more than it receives in the form of sanctity and strength. As has been said by the Sages: "Man's Sabbath expresses his week." The day of rest is not other than the Seventh Day; by itself it is nothing.

In the passage "Let me see your countenance (mirror)" (Song of Songs 2:14), there is the metaphor of the soul descending into the body, which blocks its further progress, contains it so that it is hidden, and then discharges it to return to its source. The body is the mirror receiving the light of the soul and reflecting it back in accordance with its own capacity, the heaviness of its coating, the density or smoothness of its "reflecting" surface, and the like. If the body acts as a well-made mirror, it will give forth more light than was originally received. And this is said to be the purpose of the descent of the soul into the body.

In a different context, it is written: "And the Lord God (YHVH Elohim) made coats of skins for Adam and his wife and clothed them" (Genesis 3:21). This clothing both conceals and reveals something, becoming a source of a returning light. As is mentioned in the writings of the Kabbalah, the direct light strikes reality boldly but the returning light hits against reality in a different way, illuminating in another place and another way. Which hints at a profound truth: that there are two kinds of reality, one revealed (or obvious) and one hidden (or secret)–sun and shield. Each has separate functions, and one function of the shield, the "hidden" reality, is to create shadows.

As with the mirror, the concealment (obstruction) serves as an instrument for the effulgence of a returning light. It is the hiddenness that creates the returning light, and this returning light has a magnification, an increment that does not exist in the direct light. From this we ascertain why the name YHVH Elohim assumes its other meaning–that of the concealment as a withdrawal (Tzimzum), the hiddenness as necessity. The concealment is now seen as a source of light, the origin of another dimension of reality. Thus we have a world, not of light and darkness but of direct light and returning light. This is the great truth of existence, the actuality of man "against" (confronting) that which is against him. The "against" is nothing but the manner in which returning light is reflected.

4

Division and Completeness

The first two blessings of the marriage ceremony are "Blessed is the Creator of Man" and "Blessed is the Creator of Man in His image." The Talmud (Masechet Ketubot) explains this seeming repetition as a description of the fact that the first human being, Adam, was created twice – first as a complete androgynous person, then as a divided couple, man and woman. The word "zela" (rib) from which Eve was supposedly made, may also be defined as a side (of a structure), so the female human composite was simply separated from the male. The word "naser" (to saw apart), which describes this separation, has many metaphysical implications in Kabbalistic language; one is the division of the Sefirah of Malchut (kingdom) and the subsequent coming into being of the world that we know. The creation of the first man was thus done in two stages: first the whole human being containing both the active and the passive, and then the severance into male and female.

This sawing in two creates a real separation, a distance between the parts of that which was once one and the subsequent problematics of two different personalities. It also creates a new tension, something new that had not existed before. This tension between the two who had once been a unity corresponds to the entire system of Creation: spirit and matter, higher world and lower world, direct light and returning light, and so on. These opposites reflect the fact that even though a unified world undoubtedly has great advantages, it is rather static and perhaps even uninspiring in its inability to get beyond itself, whereas a divided world is much more dynamic and capable of change. The relations between man and woman are thus part of the inner dynamics of the world.

And perhaps, at least for the sake of the literary imagination of humanity, it's just as well that this is so. For besides the need for novels and stories, there is the need for separation, and not only of the sexes, in order for creative tension to be generated. In the Kabbalah it is known as the secret of the cleavage, "Sod HaNisirah," which has its origin in the very first stages of Creation when the firmament was made, to separate the waters, forming the upper waters and the lower waters, with the eternal tension between them.

Much more of this same character was created "in the beginning," and thus, for example, the emergence of Malchut (Realm of human life) is also the separating out of an independent entity from a previous form of existence. The broken sounds of the shofar horn on Rosh Hashanah (New Year's Day) also expresses this breaking up or sawing apart of wholeness in order for something new to come into being.

Among others, there was thus formed the Written Torah

and Oral Torah, on the pattern of Adam and Eve. The Written Torah corresponds to the Sefirah of Chochmah (Wisdom) in the Kabbalistic Tree of Life, while the Oral Torah is connected to Binah (Understanding).

It will not be a digression to touch on the nature of Higher Wisdom as a source of Knowledge. Wisdom is a luminous flash in the mind, a point or instant that as yet has no extension. It provides the essential insight and is the nucleus of all knowing, not yet knowledge in terms of detailed information. Only afterwards does Understanding clothe this insight with the length and breadth of reason and make it comprehensible and communicable. The nucleus has to acquire form in order to be a recognizable "face," and this is the work of Binah.

The process is not unlike conception and giving birth: the original fertilized cell contains all, but it has to be lodged in the womb and developed. First there is only the potential, the promise and the entirety of the essence of what will be – the original source which is Wisdom. Then there is the necessary development and extension, which is Understanding.

Many Sages have claimed that the man of Understanding exceeds the man of Wisdom, because the wise person only grasps something that exists while the understanding person comprehends one thing from another. On the other hand, it has been noted that only wisdom is truly creative, that it is the origin of things. But Wisdom, in this sense, only receives the illumination. There seems to be a reversal of the passive and active roles, with Chochmah (which is male) being passive in its receptivity and Binah (which is female) being active in its task of developing the seed and issuing the product.

Of course, there are many exceptions to the rule, on the whole; however, most people have a substantial degree of understanding. Given an idea, they can extend it and apply it. Indeed, this seems to be the basis of the thinking process. On the other hand, there are people who do not seem able to develop an idea at all, and this occurs at both ends of the thinking process – from a lack of capacity or from too much brilliance. That is, some individuals get flashes of brilliant insight but are unable to do anything with them (even so-called creative people can be so handicapped), and some people can only develop or add to given ideas.

The history of thought is largely the inexplicable relations between Chochmah and Binah; between the wise ones, who are often unable to develop their own insights, and the understanding ones, who are often too busy to let a new idea enter their heads. Of course there are also people who can function on both levels, able to receive original insights and to make good use of them.

One of the problems of men of genius is the limited nature of inspiration. In the sciences, such as physics, original thinkers seem to have an effective life-span like that of football players; most of their original work is done at an early age. To be sure, a whole lifetime may be necessary to expand and develop a single flash of such enlightenment.

This many-sided relationship between Chochmah and Binah also characterizes the Written Torah and Oral Torah. It is self-evident that the revelatory nature of the Written Torah is of the nature of Chochmah. The Oral Torah, however, has many facets. A prominent part was played by Rabbi Akiva, who explicated and explained every "kotz" or detail of Halachah law and custom, under the assumption that they were not sufficiently revealed. He built a system of rules based on new disclosures, on reasoning, and on additional or qualifying opinions. Wisdom may indeed be seen as the wholeness, the entire structure of thought, but its essence lies in a certain core of perfection or truth that requires amplification. And this extension, even application, is already of the nature of Binah. It is not necessarily an increase in clarity or precision; it is a development of the original idea.

The Written Torah comes to us with letters, which are the foundation stones, and with "Tagim," or tiny increments or "crowns" to some of the letters, "Nekudot," or marks indicating how the text should be read, and "Taamim," or musical notes indicating how it should be chanted. These additional elements indicate ever higher modes of grasping the meaning of the text. Wondrous secrets are thus encompassed in both revealed and hidden features of Torah.

That is to say, the Written Torah needs endless amplification, study, and clarification. There are infinite layers of meaning, depthless beauty, and new modes of experientially living that which was revealed.

In another context of thinking, the Written Torah can be likened to a seed that can grow into a whole organism, like a tree or a person. For instance, the Torah injunction to keep the Sabbath holy was expanded into a huge volume of the Talmud, and on it many books were written. Perhaps for this reason, among others, the Torah is called Chavah (Eve), the mother of all life. It gives birth to much that in turn is the source of other products of mind and spirit. There is also the factor of emergence from the hidden, the bringing forth after an embryonic period of gestation.

It is written, "Day to day will He express speech and night to night will He manifest knowledge" (Psalms 19:2), which may indicate that each day the Written Torah will reveal itself, being of the essence of daylight, while the Oral Torah, corresponding to the darkness, is appropriate to the night. The key word is "yabia," to express or issue forth, like water gushing from a fountain or light emanating from a fixed source. The source (of Written Torah) is here Higher Wisdom, which is the revelation of Infinite Light. Pouring forth from the source, it is concentrated like a flash of lightning. It then flows in rivers of Binah (Understanding), becoming available to the requirements of life and mind as Oral Torah.

One can receive the Written Torah only passively. One who receives the Oral Torah, however, proceeds to act on it, engaging in creative thinking, deep experiencing, and specific behavior. And unlike the Written Torah, which is not given to change, erasure, or adjustment, the Oral Torah can be altered and improved and is constantly being enlarged, added to, re-created, and enhanced by ever higher levels of experience. That is, the day is the time for receiving the light, and the night is the time for creating. There is a time to perceive, to look out and absorb things, and there is a time to develop what has been absorbed and even to fashion new things out of this knowledge. It is in some ways like the photographic cycle—an instant of absorbing the light and a dark-room process of development.

Such is then the fundamental relation of Chochmah and Binah – like day and night – the time of the issuing forth of speech and the time of the development of knowledge. This is why traditional scholars usually studied Bible or Written Torah by day but Talmud and Kabbalah by night.

In another context, the two are compared to Adam and Eve. The question is asked, when were the first children conceived, in the Garden of Eden or afterwards? The Ramban claims that with the loss of the Tree of Life mankind lost their chance at eternal life through immortality and gained eternal life through the sexual experience, a "fair" exchange of personal immortality for the endless re-creation of offspring.

This notion brings us back to the sawing apart of the original Adam to make the two. The purpose was to bring forth the hidden potential in man. To be sure, the original Adam was self-sufficient and complete. The cleavage created a tension that was the beginning of a process, full of pain and sorrow but also of a new creation. This creative possibility belonged to the basic structure of Chochmah and Binah.

On the other hand, it is maintained that Chochmah and Binah are not essentially separate but rather two mutually exclusive elements of the same substance. It is in fact true that at the moment of creation there is no way of developing and that the time of developing is not the occasion for new ideas. That is, the matter of separation seems very necessary at first sight – higher waters and lower waters, day and night, Adam and Eve – but creation is not a one-way process. There is room for interaction between two opposites in order to complete Creation and bring something else into being. Thus the original Adam had to be perfect, being made by God in His image, but this perfection was not enough. The only resolution was the Messiah. A process of creation had to be initiated by which a Messianic perfection, even higher than Adam, could be achieved. Thus the meaning of separation – of Eve's being formed from the rib (the other side) of Adam – and such seems to be the purpose of the world, to manifest that which will be higher than the original.

III

THE TREE OF KNOWLEDGE

5

The Fruit of the Tree of Knowledge

The Bible story of the Tree of Knowledge of Good and Evil is familiar enough. What is less known is the varied and often opposing views of the Sages who endeavored to explain it. They wondered, for instance: What precisely was the fruit of the tree? None of the Sages said it was an apple. Some maintained that it was the grape, the potent fruit of the vine. Others were convinced, for very good reasons, that it was the fig. And still others argued in favor of the bread-providing grain, while some were even able to prove that it had to be a pomegranate. Indeed, with the spread of the Bible to exotic lands, there were those who claimed the banana to be the only conceivable fruit of the Tree of Knowledge.

The real problems, however, are more profound. If man's superiority to the animal kingdom rests on his mental capacity, if his uniqueness and glory are so largely the result of his cunning use of knowledge, why should God forbid him to eat of the Tree? What is there about knowledge that is so dangerous and terrible? As it is written, "On the day you eat of it, you will die" (Genesis 1:17).

Another intriguing question concerns the snake. How did he know that "On the day you eat of it your eyes shall be opened and you shall be as gods, knowing good and evil?" One even wonders why Eve did not ask him, "Why don't you eat of it yourself?" And it is difficult to deny that the serpent spoke the truth and was really a rather superior being, able to comprehend matters that were beyond the grasp of man. Furthermore, the Tree was critically meaningful only for man; no other creature, whether higher or lower, seems to have been interested or able to react. As God said with some concern: "Lest man be like one of us, knowing good and evil" (Genesis 3:22).

From this passage we may surmise that knowing good and evil is a heavenly quality belonging to the angels and other celestial beings and not, as we have come to believe, an earthly quality. That is, angels are not so innocent as we think, or at least their innocence is not, as with us, a function of ignorance. Their knowledge is of a different order. It is that of the encompassing Light.

In this light, the good and evil are not mixed and obscured. Each is clearly identifiable. What is more, in the encompassing Light, the good and the evil do not even contaminate each other. And not only is there no combining and blending as on earth, the celestial beings who "know" are not in the least affected by their knowledge.

Man's knowledge, however, which comes from the forbidden fruit of the Tree, is of the aspect of the inner light, and he knows good and evil only as a mixture of the two. They are hopelessly jumbled in a medley of both. The good and the evil keep influencing each other and drawing upon

54

each other for sustenance; one may even change into the other, but there is always a duality. It is man who is the decisive factor. As an illustration we may point to the ink blots of Rorschach tests. We can easily make out the dark stains from the white background; if we perceive a figure, however, then there is no longer such a distinguishing of black and white; the perceived figure prevails. And this image is something added; neither the eye of the angel nor that of a mechanical device can detect it.

But of course the matter is not a wholly subjective matter as this, or any other illustration, might imply. There are also objective factors, many of them invisible to man and not given to his control. Even in the most superficial terms, any perception is a mixture; a sense reaction is never absolutely pure; it is almost impossible to separate it from other sense impressions or from the consciousness that registers it. Not only do smells, tastes, appearances, and tactile feelings intrude on one another, but preconceptions, memories, and anticipations are influences beyond subjective control.

Evil, then, is not necessarily ugly or repellent. A vast number of demons are attractive, even genuinely beautiful. Many are extremely useful. The screens we put up to keep them out of sight are sliding and mobile walls, scarcely able to keep up with reality. All of our existence is mixed.

For man, then, the knowledge of good and evil is an awareness of, and an involvement with, a complexity that he generally cannot hope to overcome, at least in one lifetime. Only the angels seem to "know" properly. Only an encompassing awareness can keep good and evil separate and distinct, not by a mental effort of course, but as a natural consequence of the higher Light from above that does not enter into but enfolds and contains. By this light we can, for example, point out the exact moment when the sanctity of the Sabbath begins and when it ends. We can distinguish the holy from the profane. And this in spite of the undeniable existence of twilight, the in-between period when one day merges into the next. As for the inner knowledge, it has its own valid and necessary way of uniting with an object; it cannot, however, eliminate the obscurity of "twilight" situations.

To be sure, there are many additional factors. Almost all perfumes, for example, require at least one ingredient with a disagreeable odor in order to obtain the desired effect. The frankincense used in the rituals of the Holy Temple had to be blended in a very specific way with a measure of its opposite. Pure frankincense is not pleasant in itself; it is only when combined in the proper proportion with other ingredients that a powerful effect results. Ten holy ingredients mixed with the shell to the one pure frankincense without an outer shell, eleven in all. This number is itself special, one more to ten, an addition to a certain wholeness. The ten are only sparks of holiness within a shell, and they are not necessarily agreeable scents. The important thing is that frankincense has a unique quality of its own and is not dependent on any inner relation. Hence its life-giving power.

In all art, perhaps, there is a need for contrast to bring out the beauty. In addition, the contrasting element provides a means for establishing connection. Totally pure elements persist as "encompassing" factors; they do not provide anything for other factors to grab hold of. As in the material world, the more perfect a surface, the more smooth and slippery it is, the less does it offer to one's clutch. As scientists know, chemical elements with a complete number of electrons seem to be inert and do not easily combine with other elements. Even in human nature, an excess of wholeness and purity gives a feeling of being sterile in the sense that the evil finds it difficult to gain a hold. That is, the result is sometimes of questionable value and whatever creativity emerges is of a different order. Everyone else may enjoy a dirty joke, but the guileless and innocent listener does not get the point.

In the same way, it might be said that the angels remain unaffected by their knowledge of evil; they just don't get the point. Man, however, cannot know evil without becoming contaminated by it. Because his knowledge is of the aspect of the inner Light, it becomes part of his essence, what he learns becomes part of his very self. Who can say with utmost sincerity that he has met something that leaves absolutely no impression on him? Whatever a person gets to know changes him. Unlike a computer, which can contain lots of information and erase it entirely from memory and from itself, as though nothing had ever been there, a person whose consciousness absorbs something, no matter how trifling a sight or a sound, can never obliterate it as though it had never happened. This is in contrast to the reaction in the king's palace to the entry of a house-lizard. Odious as the creature may be, it cannot be totally kept out but it has no effect whatsoever on the palace. In the aspect of the encompassing knowledge, evil can be just like a house-lizard in a king's palace. It is a knowledge of something outside one's actual existence. And there is no interaction with it.

Thus, after committing what has been called the sin of

eating the fruit of the Tree of Knowledge of Good and Evil, man is no longer the same. He has to go off on another way, one of struggle and suffering and death. The innocence cannot be recovered and "meaning" has to be given to life. The angel has no such obligation imposed on him; he can know good and evil and remain an angel. When man gets to know good and evil, he can only with difficulty remain a man.

The very existence of Evil is parasitic; it depends on goodness for its sustenance. It therefore builds a sort of common life with the good and will even strive to bring sanctity into this common life. Indeed, evil flourishes best when it has the advocacy of the holy behind it. As said, the encompassing Light itself cannot make contact with the evil, but in the aspect of the inner Light evil finds the smallest crack or opening in a truth and lodges itself there, so that the lie grows within the truth. All distortion needs the straight in order to be itself.

Moreover, there are many kinds of evil, as there are of good. Not all of them have the same weight, of course, and a considerable number of persons are left relatively indifferent to many of them. Most people, in fact, have nothing in them that allows more perverse kinds of evil to take hold, so the knowledge of them remains external. When evil is in the domain of the "other," the altogether foreign, it is possible for a person to remain unconcerned. We can calmly observe violence toward an unidentified "object," but as soon as this object is recognized as a human being, especially someone we know, the reaction is very different. Compassion seems to be a function of the mind as well as the heart. This is more evident in children, in whom empathy is usually limited to the close and familiar.

There is more than one kind of knowing. One can know a whole book by heart without being able to relate to anything in it. It remains in the realm of encompassing knowledge, as a relation to the whole, not the parts. This gestalt grasp may be considered a higher knowledge, but it is also distant, and therefore wanting in some way. Since such comprehension does not have much influence, it cannot do much harm but remains pure information, exterior and largely mental. With the celestial beings, this encompassing knowledge is of a different order, but it still tends to be inactive. It does not lend itself to investigation or analysis. With inner knowledge, on the other hand, one can penetrate to deeper understanding; one can analyze the contributing elements and come to the basic building stones and the capacity to build new structures.

The inner knowledge of good and evil allows for no respite. The involvement of one with the other can become stormy; what is worse, the turbulence can become petrified into a solid mixture. In all instances man usually suffers from this interaction. He becomes personally immersed. Of course, one may ask: Can there not be a genuinely objective knowing? What about scientific observation and the power of mathematical formulae? Modern science has itself come to the conclusion that laboratory instruments have an effect on the experiment. The observations are incapable of remaining outside the gathering of knowledge. As a result, we have no pure or infallible knowledge of anything, and what we claim to know of good and evil is certainly fragmentary and subjective.

So it is with man and knowledge. Since man is incapable of maintaining more than a glimpse of encompassing Light, his awareness is always colored. But even if encompassing knowledge is fragmentary in terms of time, even if we cannot analyze it, it is emotionally integral. We can, with our senses, be aware of situations, people, moods, and experiences that are not given to intellectual explanation. But once we internalize it or relate to it, it becomes something else and there is interaction with it. In the Hebrew language, at least, the very word "to know" is linked to a variety of other modes of experience. There is always an emotional element. And there is an element that we may call communion, with all the shades of meaning that are evoked by this concept. In any case, knowing suggests a certain relation–and the absolutely cold, intellectual abstract sense of the term hardly exists. Thus for example, in the same Bible chapter telling of the Tree of Knowledge of Good and Evil, mention is made of the fact that "Adam knew Eve, his wife."

Why indeed was this distinction between encompassing and inner knowledge so important to the Chasidim? For one, it served as a guide in establishing relations. What should be the right relationship in a particular circumstance? The life of faith, for example, should be dominated by way of encompassing, by way of the congregation or the community in which one dwells. When one is thus within the community, every influence is general, not given to specific definition. One does not measure how long or where one sat in the group, but one feels the songs that were sung, the food and good cheer and inspiration that were absorbed. Even if one does not recall the details or understand the sermon, the influence is greater than can be realized. To be sure, there is the internalizing influence also, the need to understand and be intensely aware of everything. Chabad Chasidism itself is such a definite intellectualizing way. Although it does not negate the encompassing light, it emphasizes the internalizing knowledge.

There is also God's statement about Abraham, "For I have known him that he will command his sons and his house after him" (Genesis 18:19). As Rashi and other exegists explain: To know someone is to love him. This love is a deeper bond than any mental act of awareness. It is true also that when a person knows evil he is not only never again the same, the evil has become a part of him. It does not matter what he may feel about it, whether he rejects it or embraces it; the knowing is of the essence of "uniting with," and the knower must bear the consequence.

To penetrate further into the nature of the two kinds of knowing, let us recognize that an emotional grasp is also a way of wholeness, a way of seeing an object in a certain entirety for oneself, while the objective or scientific comprehension is being certain about the details, knowing what it is made of. The difference between the poet who gazes at a flower, admiring its beauty, and the botanist who counts the petals is a difference in what one is looking at as well as in the emotional diversity.

The philosophical question hinted at here is whether the analytic view is indeed that which brings us to a genuine synthesis that we may call the truth of the object, or whether an intuitive grasp of the wholeness of the object is not a more valid starting point. The answer, of course, depends on the practical requirements, and the problem has to be eternally renewed. The encompassing and the inner aspects of knowledge have to remain separate and also to complement each other. On one hand, the encompassing reality is the basis of this world and the inner knowledge is the basis for the next world. On the other hand, we claim that the encompassing is beyond the inner; the whole remains primary, greater than its parts.

Let us consider another oversimplified image to illustrate this point: a house as encompassing, food as inner reality. Food (related to the "eating" of the knowledge of good and evil) is digested and absorbed. The house never becomes a part of oneself, although it does exert influence as an atmosphere, or outer force, even of the most subtle.

We have already noted that man absorbs good and evil as inner reality, whereas to the angel they are encompassing reality. The more externalized, the less interaction. Certain things can be so utterly exterior, or encompassing, that they can be related to with utter objectivity and no interaction. A geometrical figure, for example, can be studied with great ease and accuracy. But once a scientist leaves the limited world of the visible and enters the subatomic world, interaction becomes inevitable and he can no longer observe without interfering.

Also, the closer the object of examination to our humanity, the more likely the interaction. (A physician will not treat a member of his family.) The angel on the other hand, can retain the encompassing view in any situation. It is man who gets so involved that objectivity is almost inevitably tainted, and yet there can be no denying his ability to distinguish between the encompassing and the inner view of reality. Thus, we easily realize the difference between a reckoning of another person's accounts and one's own. The adding machine does not react to the plus or the minus signs. But the scope of human error grows with the degree of involvement.

There are levels of truth that a person should not try to reach in the realm of objective knowledge, because once something is perceived it can never be dismissed. One cannot make believe that he is totally ignorant of the evil; sin "lurks at the door" forever. Innocence cannot ever be restored; all the wealth and wisdom of the world cannot buy it. A mature person can certainly remain good, and even pure perhaps, but he cannot remain innocent. Only an angel can do it, because his knowledge of good and evil is wholly external, being of the encompassing order. For man, the knowledge of good and evil becomes his beginning. He is only partly enlightened, only beginning to become like "one of us," the celestial beings.

6

The Inwardness of Evil

A passage in the *Tanya* speaks of the paradoxical way in which a person who grasps something with his understanding encompasses, and is encompassed by, the material he is studying. Merely by dealing with any subject, one is in it and out of it at the same time. To know is therefore a many-faceted experience, being, as it is, of the inner aspect.

Man thus cannot separate himself from what he knows, and though he distinguishes the good well enough, what he has imbibed causes conflict. Indeed, it is a veritable war that is initiated by the act of knowing, like the strife of the twins in the womb of Rebecca, wife of the Patriarch Isaac: "And the children struggled together within her" (Genesis 25:22). When the struggle against evil is no longer a battle against the outside, when it becomes an internal one, the nature of it changes to civil war. In such a situation, there is an obfuscation of frontiers between good and evil, even if there is no dimming of the clear distinction between the two, and so it becomes difficult to maintain contact with what is right. Indeed, the true Tzadik is the only one who can so completely cut himself off from the evil that there is no possibility of temptation, great or small.

The complete Tzadik detests evil totally; he can look upon evil without any soul intervention. The incomplete Tzadik, on the other hand, says: "I cannot hate evil with a total hatred because I myself have some evil in me." There is always an ambivalent attitude to the evil that one is not attracted to but to which attention has been drawn. Only the complete Tzadik can go anywhere, talk to anyone, without the evil in any way touching him, even though he may be able to distinguish an evil person. The incomplete Tzadik, even when he himself is incorruptible, has to struggle against evil because the war is within as well as without.

The difficulty lies precisely in the combination of inner and outer conflict. All through history, there have been generations when the evil seemed subdued and generations when it was rampant. The struggle is always with a different reality, and it is incessant, until that "day that we have waited for Him that He should save us" (Isaiah 25:9). Even the heroic man who has been able to defeat the outer manifestations of evil will discover subtleties so intricately interwoven into his personality that only with the intervention of the Lord of the Universe could he hope to get rid of them. It is not unlike a disease that continues to grow in the body and be a source of danger even after it seems to be wholly cut out.

One might ask why the achievements of a particular generation did not remain fixed at a certain level. After all, this is the way for change to occur. But there was always a residue that sprang up like a seed that had been sown in an earlier generation. For instance, King Hezekiah did right in the name of the Lord and his generation was blessed, but his heir, King Menashe, despite an exemplary education, did what was evil in the eyes of man and God so that his generation paved the way for disaster.

True, the process works both ways. One also knows good and one is unable to separate oneself from it. Thus it is impossible to find a wholly wicked person; some good necessarily clings to him. For the good cannot be uprooted entirely. Indeed it is this very condition in man of knowing good and evil that is a nucleus, not only of conflict but also of creativity.

We have already seen how the sin of knowing good and evil is a result of man's getting involved with the evil as soon as he becomes aware of it, so that it is a great struggle to separate from it. There is more here than ideas. As it is written: Adam and Eve were naked and were not ashamed. Only after eating of the fruit of the Tree did they know that other natural functions were structured in the rhythm of biological necessity, but sexuality was different, and somehow shameful. Man thereafter had to grapple with it with the aid of taboos, inhibitions, and severe social restraints. These were only partly effective in keeping the impulse under control, because, as said, the knowledge had became a part of man's being and could not be rooted out.

What is being suggested here is that evil is not simply a sum of certain drives and impulses but is the result of man's inability to separate himself from the corrupting effect of "knowing." It is like the consequences of realizing that one can get away with a lie. So long as – like in nature – it is inconceivable for a wrong action to succeed, there is no danger in multiplying knowledge. But once man learns the power of untruth, that it is possible to satisfy his desire with a lie, this knowledge can be disastrous.

Evil in itself is therefore not dangerous. It is the knowledge, the interiorizing of evil, that makes for corruption. Just as some substances are injurious to the body and others can be swallowed without harm, evil is an indifferent substance for the angels but dangerous to man. It is for this reason that God did not want man to eat of the Tree; He wanted man to be holy and avoid the terrible inner struggle of sin, the historical chain of rising and falling.

But the question remains: Why was God troubled by the possibility of Adam's taking of the Tree of Life? After all, immortality had been granted to man in the beginning. The answer, according to Sages such as the Ramban, is that everything has its time, and that in order to relate to certain things properly one must be mature enough to recognize and avoid their harmful influences. To try to relate before that invites sickness and disaster. The first man, early man, was still too immature to be like "one of us." Perhaps the "end of days" refers to the time when the spirit of uncleanness will pass from the earth. If we can go through the trouble and sorrow of this world, we may reach that stage of being in which the knowledge of good and evil will have no power to influence us and we will be like the celestial beings. In the beginning, God wished to save us from the throes of the war within us. Failing this, He had to prevent Adam from eating of the Tree of Life.

And yet the question persists: If the Tree of Knowledge is the Tree of Death why didn't God let Adam eat of the Tree of Life as a cure? It seems, from the Bible text, that God was concerned lest Adam take of the Tree of Life, whose root is of the aspect "beyond the 'shattering of the Vessels' " and live forever. In this event, there would be no way of fulfilling the greater purpose of life, which includes God's reward and punishment. If man were to exceed himself, by even one stage of being, he would be beyond the reach of justice. "If thy transgressions be multiplied what doest thou unto him. If thou be righteous what givest thou him?" (Job 35:6–7).

To better grasp this point, let us contemplate the fact that there is also a world in which good and evil do not play a role, a world in which all that exists is equal and neither evil nor good has meaning. This world is beyond the frontiers of good and evil. In human life, atonement and repentance point to such a world. In other words, there is a limit to the reality of that which breeds evil, as it is written "Evil shall slay the wicked" (Psalms 34:22). In fact, evil leads to death, so the evil impulse and the angel of death can be seen as the same entity.

The concept of repentance is a recognition of the possibility of crossing the frontier, eluding the rigid consequences, and moving to a domain beyond that of cause and effect, sin and consequences. The deeper the sin, the more powerful the repentance needed to correct it. In this world beyond, it is possible to rewrite all of history. The act of repentance is the rewriting of one's past life. He who fully repents judges his past deeds and even transforms his iniquities into virtues.

71

Atonement is yet another matter. The Day of Atonement, Yom Kippur, is said to be outside the other days of the year, beyond the calendar and the reckoning of time. The essence of Atonement is a revelation of a dimension beyond this world. In that dimension, all that was erased is transformed and gets another face. This transformation is of the aspect of the Tree of Life. In it, the sinner can rise to a level where he can fuse his being with that unchanging essence where good and evil no longer have any effect on him.

It is said that nothing can withstand the power of repentance. Therefore there is no sin so great that a person cannot make repentance for it, no past that cannot be changed. For all the merciful goodness thus manifested, one may well protest: It's not fair! A person can selfishly enjoy indulgence and vice and then choose to repent and have all his sins wiped out. He could get away with it, saying to himself while enjoying his transgressions: It's all right, I'll repent tomorrow.

The experience of repentance, however, is far more profound and just. First of all, for most repentants the weakening of the evil impulse is accompanied by a weakening of the vital force needed for repentance itself. Therefore, it is seldom possible to accomplish the full correction of the past; there are innumerable subtle and yet powerful elements that prevent an easy undoing of sin. Second, there is the truth of the prohibition against eating of the Tree of Life. In life, itself, there is a turning sword wielded by the cherubim closing the way back to immortal happiness. As for mortal happiness, one cannot transgress and clean it up with a little contrition and the performance of a mitzvah, and then go

72

back to transgression with a lively hope of thus being able to continue indefinitely. It is only theoretically perhaps that nothing stands in the way of repentance. Practically speaking, the thought of being able to "sin and repent" constitutes a serious obstacle. To be sure, the wisdom writings do say that even such a one (who intends to get away with it) can eventually achieve a genuine repentance. The fact is that the two-edged sword turning this way and that substantially prevents it.

Theoretically, of course, tasting the fruit of the Tree of Life should be as easy as eating of the Tree of Knowledge. In reality, the cherubim that prevent a person from following the untroubled path of deliberate sin and repentance may be the same force that keeps the wicked from repenting even at the very gates of Hell. And the common denominator in these two seemingly opposite attitudes is the prohibition against plucking the fruit of the Tree of Life and thereby getting at the cure for the agony of sin. The Tree of Life does not cure the sickness of the Tree of Knowledge, it only obstructs the consequences. The evil continues to exist and consequently the world does not attain redemption at the hand of man.

That is to say, evil can be overleaped by eating of the Tree of Life and entering a higher world "beyond good and evil," but this world would still be unredeemed. To redeem the earth, evil has to be overcome by confrontation and struggle, by sorting out and purification, by the conscious effort of repentance. Hence the commandment prohibiting man from eating of the Tree of Life.

To explain this point further, let us say that there are two ways of defeating the evil that is ingrained in the reality of our lives. One is by choking its growth, not allowing it nourishment, isolating it from all contact, as in the Garden of Eden. The other way is the far more complicated way of struggle after the evil has been released into the Garden. Once the evil has spread, then death works its inevitable havoc. The spirit of evil is not so easily removed from the earth after man knows sin. Great struggles, long-lived, involved, and desperate, characterize man's history.

An ancient analogy provides a graphic description. A garden is surrounded by a fence and the evil beasts are outside. Man's job is to watch over the garden and to patrol the fence so the wild beasts do not enter. But once the fence is broken and the evil penetrates, his task is to fight the beasts, both those already in the garden and those outside trying to enter. Were the man permitted to make his escape, the garden would be abandoned and go to ruin. Hence man is not so easily allowed to get out of his responsibility. He has to stay on earth, continue to care for the garden, and try to get rid of the evil he has himself introduced.

7

Banishment from Eden

From the foregoing it is evident that the Tree of Life is not the cure for the harmful results of eating of the Tree of Knowledge of Good and Evil. It would only make it possible for the evil thus let loose to last indefinitely, like the forgiveness of a sin that is not really atoned for. What is required is Tikun, the correction of evil. And for Tikun to take place, in order for the evil to be overcome, a completely different way has to be taken.

As it is written in the *Zohar,* Rabbi Acha of Kfar Tarsha tried to atone for some pestilence in a village and to purify the place by burning incense. He was told that doing so was to no avail because the people had not made amends, there had been no Tikun. Had they repented, the incense offering would have atoned. Otherwise it would be like a cleansing or purging of the effects but not of the evil itself – a healing of the symptoms and not the sickness.

God sent Adam forth from the Garden to till the soil from which he had been taken, work that requires sorting out, sowing, plowing, and harvesting. In order to be able to live from the earth, man has to keep digging, weeding, and drawing forth from the ground. The point is that the work of weeding out the harmful and proliferating the good can be done only in and with earth itself. The war of man against thorns and thistles, insects and rodents, is an incessant struggle, and it is part of his work of Tikun, correcting the world.

However, the task of building, planting, and beautifying the earth is only part of the work of "Berur," of selection and cleansing. Man also has the enormously difficult task of spiritual sorting out. It is not enough to sow and harvest the fruits of the earth; man is also enjoined to give thanks, to say blessings from the heart. Just as man eats of the products of his toil on the earth he has also to raise everything up to a higher level, restoring what he receives to its source. This too is part of the process of sorting out.

The Sages speak of the double value of working the land. On one hand, as everyone who has ever done real farming knows, one has to become subjugated to the soil in order to be able to eat from it. It is said in the Talmud that there is no more menial labor than that of the land; it is a total subordination, an enslavement. On the other hand, man cannot feel a sense of belonging, of proprietorship, of stability, and tranquility until he returns to the soil. His connection to the earth is an essential feature of life. In addition to its being the place of his origin and his ultimate return, it is where he arranges and cleans out, where he selects and cultivates the good and struggles against the bad. The earth is man's battlefield against evil.

As we know, however, this process is the bitter alternative, the only other way of fulfilling the Divine Will, necessary only after the fruit of the Tree of Knowledge was imbibed and man was cast out of the Garden. Man's task in the Garden had been simply to disseminate the Infinite Light, so that the holy sparks that had fallen were restored. That is, the original and preferable way to overcome evil was not to fight it but to provide a source of light. Instead of man's engaging in the painstaking process of sorting out the inimical, the holy sparks were drawn to the great fire and absorbed in it and what was left could not survive on its own.

As in daily life, there are two ways of sorting: One is to find and throw away the waste, the other is to select and aggrandize the edible. These are different processes halachically as well as in terms of their essence. The point is that the best way to get rid of darkness is simply to add light. The shadows vanish of themselves, and light can be shed on any subject, in any situation, by means of love. There is no need for struggle, contention, or confrontation. It is perhaps the way at the level of the Messiah, the way of peace and not war. It may be argued that there are two categories of Messiah, Messiah Ben Yosef and Messiah Ben David. But even then only the first carries out the final war. While the second, Messiah Ben David, destroys evil, not by any action on his part, but simply by being there; "being there" creates a situation in which evil cannot exist, it is nullified before Him. The world has to nullify itself before the Divine Light. But we should be aware that this is a process that happens all the time, quietly and unobtrusively.

To be sure, there is often a need for the violent alternative, to struggle, which is the constant re-entry into the self, inward, to resolve the issue. But if a person, with all his mixture of good and evil, can love something truly, if his very heart goes out to it, he can nullify himself before it without struggle. There is a point of light to which men are inevitably attracted, to which they keep giving themselves. It is the nature of light to influence by creating a whole new situation. Such manner of influence attracts the sparks. There is no need for speech. The good is drawn to the source of light. This is the process of Eden, where man just cared for his Garden, unconcerned about what was happening anywhere else.

It has been said that Israel is destined to be a light unto the nations. This task is like the action of a candle. The candle makes no effort to combat the darkness; it does not go from place to place to shed its light. Its sole function is to burn with a little flame of its own, and without ulterior motive, it casts a light which dispels shadows. Israel has no purposeful duty other than to be itself as a candle, to give forth light and let persons who are drawn to it come and become part of it.

Count Potozki was a rather famous convert to Judaism, a Polish aristocrat with lands and fortune. He was burned at the stake in Vilna and his buried ashes became a holy place. One of the many anecdotes attributed to him was his response to the frequently asked question: Dear Count, if you really wish to be a decent person, or even a religious man, we could understand, but why on earth should you want to be a Jew? His answer was based on the Midrash that the Torah was originally offered to all the peoples of

80

the earth and only the Jews accepted it. Furthermore, as it is written in the Bible, the choice remains open for all men: "Because not only with you alone do I make this covenant, I make it with those who are here this day before the Lord and with those who are not here with us today" (Deuteronomy 29:13–14). In fact, the covenant is an eternal bond with all the generations of those who choose to be of Israel. When those of the nations are drawn to the covenant, they convert; when Jews feel that they do not wish to be a part of it, they leave the fold.

From this it follows that one of the reasons for the Exile is to enable the Jews to wander among the peoples of the earth and gather up these isolated sparks. What would have happened if Israel had not been exiled? The answer given is that the sparks would have been drawn toward, and absorbed into, the great Light, like a small candle in the flame of a bonfire – like Naama the Ammonite, wife of Solomon, who was brought into the Royal House of David to be part of the chain of the Messiah, or like all those who came from afar to hear the wisdom of Solomon. If Israel merely let its splendor radiate in all directions, even the most distant lost sparks would come of themselves to Israel, each in its own way and its own time, directly or indirectly. When the Holy Temple stands on the hilltop in Jerusalem, its very existence radiates a great luminosity that exceeds the limitations of space.

So too, before the incidence of sin, man's physical existence was pure holiness. His body was taken from the place of the altar, his 248 organs were formed in the sanctity of ritual purity. He was not produced by war and strife; rather the holy sparks would find their way easily, and evil, unable to exist without the support of the good, would vanish. The problem of life, as well as of good and evil, could be resolved by itself, without strife and anguish.

But since the introduction of sin, it is necessary to sort out good and evil by work and war. As it is written in the *Zohar,* "The hour of prayer is an hour of battle." Every prayer is a part of the process of strife with reality. Even the apparently innocent factors involved in the act of prayer, or eating, involve warfare. Man's very existence, whether he is immersed in holy deeds or in the filthy affairs of the world, is a constant struggle with the essence of himself. He is constantly subjected to suffering. He strikes out and he is himself struck down in a repeated cycle of selection, of "Berur." He has to keep confronting things of this world and getting painfully involved with them. True, one may claim that in prayer one is free, for it is the soul that prays. But one cannot tell one's physical body to wait outside for an hour or so until one finishes the morning's worship. The mind can hardly be kept still for a few moments, as anyone who prays regularly knows full well. In fact, the Jews have a large stock of jokes poking fun at the uninvited thoughts that arise during the daily prayers.

Man, then, cannot be anywhere but in the world of action. It is by descending consciously into the world of the shell that he executes the process of sorting out. Instead of caring (in joy) for the Garden, as before the fall, he now has to care (in sorrow) for the earth from which he came.

And what is the origin of this sorrow, of the knowledge of good and evil that tore man out of his innocence. All indications point to the serpent. How could he know about the power of the Tree "to make one as the gods," unless he himself was of the same order. The essence of the serpent belonged to the same order as the Tree of Knowledge. One might even suggest that the serpent served as a personification of the Tree, representing something of its dual meaning for man. He was almost human in his shrewdness and intelligence, so by a slight turnabout we can see ourselves. As the *Zohar* remarks, man is clothed in the ever-changing skin of the snake. Indeed, some Sages have ventured to add that the first garments God made for man were those taken from the snake whom He had skinned and then doomed to crawl on his belly. The esoteric meaning is that the snake belongs to the kind of intelligence that brings man to eat of the Tree of Knowledge.

As we have mentioned, it may be that originally God in His mercy desired to keep man in a separate world of his own in the Garden, free from the strife and sorrow of evil and of "knowing." In this world, perfection was "natural." It seems that this world is not an illusion. It still exists, as we may surmise from certain kinds of "holiness" that keep turning up in life: a face that makes us melt, a landscape, a song, an unanticipated encounter that carries us to a dimension of joy. Furthermore, there have always been individuals who manage to remain at this level of being. Even until quite recently there have been instances of personalities who never even had to say or do anything; anyone who came near them received whatever it was he had to receive, and the result was a sense of wholeness, of perfection. In any case, we are reminded of man's state before his sin.

It would appear that the serpent, who belonged to the Tree of Knowledge, was vexed and exasperated by this immunity of man to evil. He resented not being noticed, not being related to. Adam was quite content to let everything be as it was, including the serpent, in his conflict and torment. Which only increased the resentment of the snake, so that he tried to draw man into the circle of struggle.

Consequently, man was made a part of the imperfect world and became involved in the war of good and evil. An ambivalent relation has resulted with the serpent and all that the serpent symbolized. As it is written: "Sin lies at the door and all his desire is for you and you will rule over him" (Genesis 4:7). Sin accompanies us wherever we go. We live together, the serpent and I. And though we step on him, he does not care; all he wants is to be noticed. Indeed, were man to dismiss his fascination for the serpent and turn his mind elsewhere, the serpent would lose his reason for existence and shrivel up.

Nevertheless, the words of the serpent were true: Upon eating of the fruit of the Tree of Knowledge, man knew good and evil and entered into another level of being. Perhaps it is a more complete state in that he has the freedom of choice as well as the Divine spark. This freedom is also a Divine power, making him a more dynamic factor in the universe, a more proficient partner in the process of Creation.

The serpent may have had his own mischievous reasons for tempting the man, but he was not lying. By eating of the Tree of Knowledge, man could become as the gods. This was more than just a temptation, it was a profoundly alluring prospect – to be complete, to overcome the fragmented state of his ignorance, and to know, as the gods know, the whole truth by experiencing all that there is to be experienced. How many excellent persons, throughout human history, have fallen prey to this urgent need to know, by greater or lesser intensity of experience, *all* the aspects of life, including the evil!

The serpent's cunningness was rooted in the partial truthfulness of the prospect. Man did come to know good and evil as the gods, but unlike the gods, he internalized it. The celestial beings were able to sustain an encompassing knowledge of good and evil; it never really troubled them. But man, being vulnerable to all influence, becomes so involved with what he knows that he cannot ever get rid of it.

The result, we are only too well aware, is the prevalence of the evil impulse and its concomitant inevitability of death. At the same time, this may be the factor that enables man to rise above the angels. For man is indeed a spiritual being, belonging, like the angels, to the upper worlds. He also has an inner life, which is his danger. Unable to suffice with an encompassing knowledge, having absorbed the knowledge of good and evil, he has to enter into the lower aspects of life, where he must grapple with these forces. And it is this struggle with sin, if he is successful, that enables man to rise a little above the angels.

As is noted in the Likutei Torah of the Ari, Adam, being a sublime creature, walked in the Upper Mansions and lived in the celestial spheres. And according to Rashbi, even the greatest human beings in history are not of that stature;

at best they may be able to see something of the upper worlds and make spiritual contact, but they don't "walk about" in them. Adam, walking freely, did not even bother to cast a glance at the lower worlds of uncleanness. The serpent, however, enticed him: "Take a look! There are other mansions, another place that you have not visited." So Adam faltered and, without intending to do so, "fell" into sin.

This is a slightly different version of the Bible narrative. Its description of the primordial state is more abstract, more spiritual. However, the essential factors remain: that at first Adam did not even look at these other realities, and that when he did, he could not separate himself. The only way man could avoid being involved in evil was to remain ignorant of it.

At this point let us make a slight digression and consider the character of Joseph in the Bible. The selling of Joseph by his brothers is followed by the account of Judah's journey to Adullam, where he took a woman to wife, had sons by her, and then after some grievous mishaps was seduced by his daughter-in-law, Tamar. This account is followed by the story of Joseph's service in the house of Potiphar and his repulsing the seductions of Potiphar's wife. There seems to be some message in the opposite ways taken by Judah and Joseph–the way of plunging into the world and its evils, and the way of purity, disavowing the evil of the world. Each has his own task to perform. And in the longer sequence of history, they are expressed in the two Messiahs that appear at the end of time: Messiah, son of Joseph, and Messiah, son of David (or Judah).

A similar logic seems to accompany the story of David

and Jonathan, son of Saul. Why was the kingdom taken from the house of Saul and given to David? Saul was in some respects a very saintly man; his son Jonathan was certainly a pure soul as well as a brave and perfect human being, while David had more than one side to him that succumbed to temptation. Can one conclude that too much perfection is unproductive? Is it necessary for man to "leave his brothers and turn aside to a certain Adullamite" (a stranger), to get so involved with the imperfections and unpredictable dangers of life that almost anything is liable to happen? According to the Bible, it would appear that there has to be a plunging into the fierce struggles of the world, a confrontation with good and evil. Even Joseph, who could not be a completely innocent soul like his brother Benjamin, had to go down to Egypt and there perform the act of Tikun, of restitution.

Hence Adam was sent forth from Eden. The only way to overcome the uncleanness and evil of the world was to go "down" into it and engage in constant struggle.

8

The Two Ways of Tikun

When the Sages speak of the "Duration of the Exile," what is meant is not only the historic period of Jewish exile from the Holy Land, but the state of the whole world until the Redemption. It is the time of sorting out the evil and separating it from the good. From this we may gather that the essential task of our existence in this world is the work of "Berurim," sorting out, selecting, and separating.

This work is (kabbalistically) of the aspect of Chochmah, or Wisdom. How else is it to be accomplished? "By Chochmah shall you distinguish" *(Zohar)*. Hence wisdom is also called judgment, since in every choice there is value discrimination and definition of limits.

But definition of limits is of another order of Attributes: it is Binah, or Understanding. Chochmah is the initial light of recognition, the original point of departure by which something may be grasped. Binah is the comprehension of what is grasped, that which makes it real. Chochmah is intuitive and immediate, Binah is rational and analytical. Chochmah is of the aspect of vision, Binah is of the aspect of hearing.

What is the difference between seeing and hearing? Someone tells me about a person and I thus hear about him; I then happen to see him in person. The act of seeing is a different kind of connection; it seems the more "real." Seeing, like Wisdom, is a total grasp of what is revealed; hearing, like Binah, tends to be a more distinct perception of limited scope. In many respects, then, Chochmah is the key to things, positioned on the border between the conscious and the unconscious, while the mind, or the intelligent reason, may be identified with Binah.

A closely related problem is that of Truth. Philosophers have pondered over it at great length, but the ordinary person scarcely gives it any consideration. How does one recognize the truth? According to the Sages, there are several ways of doing so, and sometimes they have to be used in combination. For example, there is the test of harmony; truth has to fit in harmoniously with reality. Another test is that of eternity, the fact that a truth lasts and does not change. Still another, far less philosophic, mark of truth is that it creates in one a click, an immediate responsiveness. This "unthinking" recognition is not incompatible with the test of harmony. The essential question remains, however: How does one know? What does one do about a contradiction or a gap, making discrimination doubtful?

The problem is that Binah cannot really provide the answer. It is itself based on a certain analytical mechanism, extremely complex at times, of distinguishing the true by eliminating the false. We are thus thrown back upon Chochmah to recognize the truth for us.

This action of Chochmah is judgmental; it is not merely

passive and indecisive. Parenthetically we may note that one can also make a distorted judgment. This does not mean that Wisdom itself is distorted or unreliable in its operation. Nevertheless it does happen that someone calls light darkness and the good evil. The process, however, is what counts, based as it is on a genuine power of discrimination.

In the long run, at least, there is a final solution. As more than one Sage claims, during the Exile, when we separate out the evil under the Sefirah of Wisdom, we are rectifying, bringing to Tikun, the level of Knowledge. We set right the effect of the Tree of Knowledge because the root of the problem is that good and evil are so mixed that they become a single essence. At the moment we separate them, the evil has no genuine existence of its own; it can continue only as a parasite. Thus when the evil is isolated, its existence is nullified of itself. There is the story of a king who used to punish those who bought from thieves more than he punished the thieves themselves. The formula is that the problem is not the mouse who steals but the hole through which he comes. Were no one to buy from the thief, the criminal underworld could be eliminated. There is no way of dealing with the evil itself. The task of Chochmah is to make the painful cut, to launch a process of Tikun, an extermination of that which sustains evil.

This brings us to a certain interesting Kabbalistic issue. The argument here presented makes Chochmah act as Din, the power to discriminate and judge, which usually belongs to the Sefirah we know as Gevurah (Strength). According to the early Kabbalists, Chochmah belongs to the right line of the Chart of the Sefirot, the line of Chesed (Grace) and of

93

Netzach (Victory). The left line is that of Gevurah (Strength or Severity) with Binah (Understanding) above it and Hod (Splendor) below, while the central line is Daat (Knowledge), Tiferet (Beauty, Harmony) and Yesod (Foundation). According to the early Kabbalists, these three lines were fairly separate and autonomous. Our present Chasidic line of argument takes issue with this approach, claiming that Chochmah is not entirely one thing or another; it has something of Din (Judgment) in it and consequently is intimately related to Gevurah. In the process of discrimination, the role of Chochmah would be to reveal, to make manifest, the True.

It is possible then, that Chochmah is not only Chesed; it is also Din, or Judgment, which is ordinarily placed in the category of Gevurah. The Ari once addressed this possibility by pointing to the passage in the *Zohar* (Idra), "Like wine that ferments on its yeast." This wine, or fermented stuff, has ultimately gone through some process of "Berur," or selection. Chochmah is qualified by a process of interaction and change that may be compared to chemical processes, which are mainly Chesed-like in their action, but it can also be compared to the fermentation of wine, which has been held as one of the symbols of Gevurah.

The act of separating out the evil is thus a matter of Din as Judgment, as a vehicle of the Attribute of Gevurah. Wherever there is Tzimzum (Divine Contraction), there is also concealment (of the Divine), and such is the quality of Din as Severity, as it is written: "Blessed is the man whom thou chasteneth, O Lord" (Psalms 94:12). For the trials and sufferings which serve to get rid of the evil by separating it out, are of the aspect of the Yod and Heh (the first of the four letters of the Tetragrammaton) and correspond to Chochmah and Binah. Why are trial and suffering a way of sorting out the evil? After all, in themselves they cannot be considered good. Otherwise one could say that suffering is inflicted on a person to sweeten or dilute his wickedness. Since suffering is of the aspect of Gevurah and also of evil, how can it sweeten the bitter taste of evil? The answer is that actually the sweetening of evil comes from within, from within Gevurah itself, the trials and sufferings merging with the evil and becoming a unity. It is a closed experience, in that nothing more can happen, because evil without suffering is an anomaly, like an evil that did not accomplish its purpose.

Another feature of evil is its insatiable thirst, a restlessness that knows no bounds. Evil can never be quiet, being always in need, incomplete, and impaired. It therefore has to fasten itself on to the good, and endeavor to draw from it that which it needs. Feeding on the good, the evil grows bigger and fatter, and more hungry. It is never really satisfied. There is no limit to the appetite of the evil impulse. It comes to an end only when it consumes itself. Like any biological disease or cellular disorder, such as a DNA deficiency or cancer, as the evil grows, it becomes worse rather than better, even if its growth is at the expense of the healthy part of the organism. Only when evil reaches a final point of saturation that casts it out of the world, only then does it come to a natural end. Its very existence is based on distortion of essence or some irregularity of function, and this very irregularity requires some sort of "fulfillment" which, when it happens, brings the whole process to a stop.

Therefore, in this respect, suffering is not only the result of evil, it is also the final resolution of evil. Like any number of dangerous processes in life that continue to grow and ripen until a certain point is reached when they no longer constitute a danger, the process resolves itself. If, however, there is any interference with the development, it is likely that the danger point will not be passed. Consequently, it would seem, the evil has to get, not to its punishment, but to its fulfillment, through suffering.

One may say that the "shell" or evil impulse in man is like the leech that sucks the blood until it dies. The leech needs the blood for its own fundamental life purpose; but when it so fulfills itself, its life cycle has come to an end and it ceases to live. However, if one removes the leech before it satisfies itself, it will remain alive and thirsting for blood. Similarly the mosquito will bite until it is full, upon which it has completed a cycle and it will die.

The same principle appears to have been behind the ritual of the scapegoat in ancient times. The goat, so chosen to represent evil, is pampered and then sent forth into the wilderness, thereby being "terminated." One has to give to the shell its due portion, as Jacob gave Esau gifts, so each could then go on his own way. If Jacob does not give a proper portion to Esau, Esau remains hungry. Evil receives sustenance from evil or from the good transformed into "food" for evil.

As it has been explained, after Adam ate of the Tree of Knowledge and became contaminated by evil, he needed to become subject to the process of sorting out, by which the sparks of holiness in him would be raised up. This would be accomplished by Chochmah (Wisdom) because Wisdom also contains something of Gevurah in the sense that God tries us with severity and suffering. But affliction can come on any number of levels, also as a resolution to something. When there is sin and there are afflictions that resolve this sin, the circle of sin is closed and the sin is no longer remembered. But when a man sins and he suffers no affliction, the sin remains lodged in reality. This sin will not have any resolution. And it will therefore grow, and keep growing all the time. It wants more.

One could say, from this point of view, that sin and suffering are one, constituting a single circle of reality. This circle is not a thing and its contradiction, but rather a thing and its completion. This particular completion, however, is negative in the sense that evil exists because of its lack of completeness. As soon as it is completed, it ceases to be anything definite. It becomes something altogether neutral, upon which it is given to treatment and to correction, to some kind of transformative action.

In a similar vein, we have Satan descending and tempting, rising up from below and working mischief, coming to us unawares and injecting vital force into the soul. Again the same circle, the circle of evil, a circle that has its own wholeness. When Satan tempts or vivifies, he thereafter requires the soul of the one to whom he has given life; the punishment that comes after the sin is in a certain sense not only the result, but the completion of the circle of evil. Whereupon, the matter comes to its own resolution. If it does not reach resolution, it has to submit to some sort of continuation.

Pursuing this line of reasoning, since man ate of the Tree

97

of Knowledge, his life became like a question without an answer. He had to be thrown into the world and to suffer in the world, doomed to do the work of selection, sorting out the good from evil. His afflictions, agonies, and sweat were all part of this work of selection, the task of correcting and overcoming the evil which he had himself assumed and from which he was somehow nourished.

The Tree of Life, on the other hand, is on the level of Keter (Crown), the Sefirah above Chochmah. Keter is also supernal compassion, in darkness as in light. Therefore there is concern lest Adam reach out and take also from the Tree of Life and live forever. This level of Keter transcends good and evil, being so total a love that it does not discriminate or relate to the receiver. There is no difference between above and below, between good and evil.

The difficulty is that man is an internalizing creature, absorbing the evil into himself and unable to separate himself from it. The evil is so deeply interwoven in his life, it can be gotten rid of only with enormous effort, or at least with that special effort called repentance. Like the incense burned by Rabbi Acha to try to purify a village that was still under the shadow of sin, the effort is to no avail without repentance.

Concerning the offering of incense, the ancient tradition saw it as a ritual means of making contact beyond the borders of physical reality. It belonged to the realm of the encompassing forces. Thus one of the main duties of the High Priest in the Holy Temple, (especially at Yom Kippur) was to burn incense to atone for the sins of the people. This contact with the beyond was crucial. It was the source of life.

We have already discussed the fact that when Adam was banished from the Garden of Eden, he was also sent to till the earth from which he was taken, to separate the good from the evil in it, the sorting out being a corrective process. Afterwards, there was the eating of the fruits of his labor, and the enjoyment of this harvest is also an act of choosing and discriminating. As in prayer, one gives thanks for the nourishment that enables one to raise the sparks of holiness hidden in the food. Because there is a circle of life in which man's place is crucial, he has to sort out things in the material world and then he is enjoined to raise that which he has selected to a higher level, even to holiness. By sanctifying his food, he is using his special relation to the Divine for this purpose of correcting the reality of the world.

To accomplish this, it was necessary to leave the Garden of Eden. That was not the place in which to sort things out. The closed circle of Eden is a glorified version of reality, a world without sin, a self-sufficient harmony of its own. This is the ideal world of the innocent, but it was not adequate for the no longer naive Adam. In fact, the whole situation suddenly became dangerous, for both man and the Garden, which he would only spoil. It was not the environment in which he could correct either himself or the world. He had to be thrown out into the world of evil, even if it meant pitting evil against evil. It was precisely by this means, of struggle and conflict, that he could fix the world, or at least introduce some order into it.

The problem that now confronted life was man's inexperience with evil. Not having known anything of evil before, how could he choose and get on with the job of selection and separation? As it is said in the Midrash: Man discovered evil before he was able to deal with it. He was not yet mature enough, his soul was not ready to negotiate or struggle with evil; on the contrary it could even destroy him.

In other words, certain things can be dealt with if one is able to fit them into some framework, but otherwise they are liable to be destructive. Man needs to be sufficiently developed in order to deal with the more profound issues of life. For the simple matters, he could have remained in Eden, but to deal with the world outside the Garden, in order to complete the world, so to speak, man had to grow up. Some Sages say this is the meaning of the phrase in Genesis at the end of the account of the Creation: "which God created, to do" (Genesis 2:3). That is, God creates a world that still has all sorts of things in it that are incomplete, and man's task is to complete them. How can man complete creation so long as he remains in the Garden of Eden?

We have already said that when man was without sin in the Garden, he carried out the task of redeeming the world, not by strife and struggle, but by allowing the infinite Light to gather up all the sparks of holiness that had become mixed up with evil. It is like the automatic snuffing out of a small flame when it is close to a large bonfire. The larger the fire and the nearer the flame, the greater the fire's power to nullify the flame. If they are too far apart, there will be no influence.

What is being described here are the two ways of overcoming evil and thereby effecting lasting change. One way is the familiar struggle of trying to put some order into a world into which we are thrown. It is a constant effort of orientation, sorting out, and getting free from a negative or painful situation. This is the result of having been cast out of the security of Eden into a world of sorrow and toil, as a punishment for sin. It parallels the sin of the golden calf after the giving of the Torah, and it parallels the destruction of the Temple and the dispersion of Israel. In every case, the sin creates a sudden break with the past and a banishment into exile. Being cast out of one's homeland into the Galut is the same as having to struggle with evil. This evil is not necessarily one's own. Man is confronted with a life-negating wrongness that is outside his own realm. He discovers that he is living with evil and the evil is living within him.

As in every war, victory is not certain. Man's struggle is very trying because it is war from within and without. Man has to struggle on two fronts at the same time, incessantly repairing himself while trying to correct the outer world. If only one of these two were sound and complete, it would be easier. Both are connected somehow in the total state of suffering and humiliation that qualifies the process of Tikun.

What would be the alternative? It would be the one originally offered to man in Eden, where the good is made so whole and complete, so great in its independence, it creates a situation of reparation and rightness by inspiration and not by war. Here there is no need to enter into things and go through the painful process of separating out the evil. One can remain withdrawn and outside the wrongness and the chaotic and let it come to its own order, fix itself. That is, if man can extinguish the candle by letting it be close to the bonfire, he does not have to snuff it out himself. If necessary, he can add fuel to the bonfire or just bring the candle nearer.

In the course of life, even in the way of struggle to correct evil, there is the alternate way of harboring the good, allowing it to grow and draw to itself all the holy sparks. As it is written: Israel was exiled in order to attract proselytes, to bring more people into the fold of Torah – that is, to augment the luminosity and the sparks of holiness. The interaction of Israel with the world draws sparks of holiness from every direction.

Had Israel not sinned and been banished into exile, this would not have been possible. Israel thus has a task in the world, to raise the holy sparks, to augment the light in the many places where darkness dwells.

True, the raising of the sparks can be accomplished without exile – by the power of attraction to a higher reality. We may take the examples of Ruth the Moabite and of Naama the Ammonite, both of whom were drawn to leave their country and to join the destiny of Israel in such a way as to make a permanent mark on that destiny. They became the "mothers" of the Messiah, joining those who gave birth to the royal line of David. Indeed Naama is said to have come to Solomon, as did the Queen of Sheba, because she had heard of his greatness and was irresistibly drawn to his light. When there is a luminous attraction, like the court of Solomon the Wise, the "spark" can come to the fire.

So just as there are centers of sickness that can spread, there are any number of modes of benevolent influence, of goodness and light. These beneficial centers also have the power to grow and draw to themselves that which comes under this influence. But this attraction requires a certain level of being, more mature and powerful than the surrounding forces. A farmer could not leave a field untilled and return expecting to find it covered with roses, or even wheat. He will more likely find it overgrown with weeds and thorns. The rose is a very pampered plant, so many things interfere with it, but the weeds have no trouble flourishing. True, there have been experiments to develop a species of wheat that would have the resilience and strength of wild wheat, able to grow in any conditions, capable even of thrusting out the weeds. But the fact is that our cultivated crops of flowers and food need more care than ever. Our Tzadikim, our men and women of virtue, need a lot of cotton wool to protect them from the environment.

It would seem, then, that only if there is some interaction is there influence. We are therefore all in exile, both the individual and the nation. These two exiles, the personal and the social, are descents for the purpose of rising, except that every such descent is accompanied by much pain, which in both cases is not necessary.

This brings us to the alternative, an augmentation of the power of the good. Were good able to become powerful, it would of itself conquer the evil. There would be no need to go out to correct the world; the world would come to man to be corrected. In the case of the Garden of Eden, Adam was perhaps too immature, too undeveloped. He could not correct the reality of the world by his very essence.

The Garden of Eden needs to be carefully watched to keep

103

Hell from making inroads into it. If the Garden were more whole and complete in the sense of being strong and unassailable, it could spread and cover the whole earth. Man's task was not only to take care of the Garden, but to make it ever more perfect and powerful enough to change all of earthly reality. Once he had sinned, he had to do the same thing in a different manner.

The task may be compared to the challenge of sickness. A healthy organism is complete and does not need anything. When sick and incomplete, it has to be treated with medicines. And as it is written in the Talmud, there is no medicine that is not harmful; it's only a matter of how much more good it does than harm. This is part of the problem of interfering with the wholeness of an organism. When one is vaccinated against disease, the inimical bacteria is injected into the blood; the principle is that the best way to fight the inimical or any evil is by using the same element of destruction. In the esoteric wisdom too there are ways of sweetening the severity of Gevurah at its root, of combating evil by another evil, poison by poison.

The point is that it is possible to come to health without the injection of bacteria, and that is by letting the innermost organism be so whole and free that the bacteria (evil) cannot penetrate. The former is artificial curing, the latter is natural health.

Man, it seems, did not want to be healthy. He ate of the Tree of Knowledge. Once he did so, the only choice was to start on the way of artificial cure and correction. One is reminded of the fact that Eskimos never knew what an ordinary cold was; once they were infected by civilized man, they had no resistance to it and they died by the hundreds.

What happened to man because of the Tree of Knowledge is not very different. He caught a cold. And indeed, what occurred was no closer to the depths of evil than a sniffling nose; it was only afterwards that man invented the subtleties and forces of corruption. But at the time it was enough for his vulnerable, innocent existence. His soul did not have any resistance against the sickness of evil.

Were he to eat of the Tree of Life, the situation would have remained static. The parasite would continue to exist but be unable to develop and cause harm. The organism would not have been able to move on to another stage, however. In order to do so, man has had to develop a higher immunity, by enduring the sickness, fighting the evil to the bitter end. By overcoming the illness, he may be said to have eliminated the evil from his own being and from the world.

We may conclude that the alternative to the life of struggle existed but was theoretical. It was theoretically a possibility for man to be able to correct himself in a positive manner, and thereby also to positively fix the reality of the world. By virtue of his capacity to sustain a higher level of being, man could spread the light from his own point of focus to the whole world. But when he sinned, he had no choice but to go about the job of putting things to right in a wholly different manner. If only Solomon had not opened the way to idolatrous worship by submitting to his wives, if only Israel had continued the original way of Solomon and had not put an end to the Glory, then perhaps this glory would have been able to spread over the entire earth. There was a crisis which ultimately resulted in the exile of Israel. And the Exile was intended to fulfill the same purpose of putting the world in order by Tikun, but through pain and sorrow.

And this way of carrying out the Tikun reparation of the world is the only way now offered to us. We may speak of the possibility of a Garden of Eden, but it is theoretical. Eden no longer exists, at least not for us. We have only the second alternative, the way of exile, the circumstance of being human and being banished from the Garden.

IV

OUTBOUND
AND INBOUND
FORCES

9

Draw Me after Thee

D raw me after thee and we shall come running" (Song of Songs 1:4). This statement opens with a plea in the first person singular and finishes with a reciprocal action in the plural. This may be explained by the fact that man has two souls. "Besides the animal soul, there is the Divine soul, whose nature it is to be drawn to, and to cling to, the blessed unique One and this for no reason or purpose." The Divine soul is indeed a spark from the Divine and needs no push or prodding to make it reach for God; it does so because that is its nature. As for the animal soul, it is familiar enough to all men, being that which is expressed by our desires and the structure of personality.

Why is the emphasis put on the uniqueness, the "one and only" aspect of the Divine, as that to which the spark of the soul aspires? Because of that quality of the soul called "self" or solitary one. This selfhood of the soul belongs to the higher soul, to the spiritual plane where there is a possibility of genuine individualization. From this we may surmise that the "oneness" is the inner kernel or basic essence of the soul from which all else follows. Furthermore, as we have seen, the soul aspires to God not out of love, but simply because it must, because doing so is its very essence. It is not an urge that can be traced to any outer influence or pressure, it is an entirely self-driven impulsion, a result of the very essence of its self which is individual and needs to be only itself.

As one of the Chasidic Sages said: "The matter can be explained by the nature of the will of the soul, which is related also to the element of pleasure; for that which is not willed will not give the soul pleasure; on the contrary, the soul will be grieved." In other words, the soul striving to God is the very will of the soul. The pleasure in realizing this wish is called "Love in delights."

Love in delights is therefore the consummation of the soul's approach to God. But it is the soul's will to God that is the basis; the pleasure is secondary. This is not the same will that may be found in other contexts, such as the animal soul; rather, the will to unite with God is identical with the very essence of the Divine soul. As it is said: The higher soul is called "Yechidah," the unique self, because it clings to the only One, and this unity with the One is not a particular quality or aspect of the soul, it is its very essence. This must bring pleasure, "for if someone does not want something he will not gain pleasure from it, but will be grieved." The pleasure comes as a consequence of the wishing, from the fulfillment of a desire.

An original view of this was expressed by Rabbi Nachman of Breslav. In the story of The Seven Beggars he said that everything in the world comes from sorrow. Man, and indeed all created things, lack something, and only when they get whatever it is they lack can they experience joy. The world and all that it contains, by being "other" than God, is in a state of unfulfillment, and the feeling of sorrow prevails in all relationships. That is to say, there is a gap in the soul, and only when the gap is filled, when the desire is satisfied, can there be joy or pleasure. This pleasure arouses and makes possible the functioning of the mind, with its intelligence and emotions. The beginning, therefore, of the whole chain of the soul's behavior is the will. All that the soul creates and fashions out of itself is a function, and expression, of what it wants.

All of the above may seem abstract, but conclusions to be drawn from it are in the area of morality. It has been indicated that the essential difference between the Divine soul and animal soul lies not in the soul's character but in the objects of its desire. If a man can reach a level where he is able to influence the nature of his desires, his animal soul will be changed and become a Divine soul. In other words, the peculiar essence of the animal soul is basically a matter of its desires. And if these desires can be changed and reversed, the animal soul is transformed into something else. What we are considering is not necessarily a sublimation of desire, raising it from a low level to a higher level. The question is: what is the object of the desire? If the object of desire can be elevated, then the development of the soul will proceed in good order. Everything depends on the nature of things to which a particular soul is drawn. If it is drawn to holiness, then much of its life will be holy.

On the other hand we are harassed by the desires of the

animal soul. It should be emphasized that the animal soul is not identical with the instincts of the body. It is human in its essence and consists of all the parts of a man except for that part which has a certain independent relationship to the Divine. The relation to the Divine – that is the essence of the Divine soul. All the rest, the human mesh, is the animal soul.

It is therefore a mistake to think of the animal soul as animal-like. It is an animal in the way that the fox is supposed to be the cleverest of animals. The former Rabbi Yoseph Yitzchak of Lyobavitch, speaking about his father's criterion for distinguishing between the good impulse and the evil impulse, said that it was simply a matter of being very precise about what a person desired. What was its basic quality? It could even be a matter of a mitzvah or deep concentration in prayer. What was it if it prevented a person from doing a real good? Could it not then be considered part of the activities of the animal soul? The rabbi added: "Till then I knew that the animal soul could be a scholar; now I learned that there could be 'a Chasid animal soul' (an animal soul parading as a Chasid)." From this it may be deduced that the problem of whether a thing is good or evil, the problem of knowing from which soul it comes, may be solved by distinguishing the desire behind it, what the soul wants at that particular moment.

Actually the soul is divided and wants different things. The Divine soul itself is said to have five spiritual levels: soul, spirit, Neshamah or higher soul, Chayah or creature, and Yechidah or unity. The animal soul overlaps, at best, only the three lower levels; it lacks Chayah and Yechidah.

114

And why is there no "unity" or Yechidah in the animal soul? Because it has no one single object of desire; because it wants different things, all of them outside of the Divine essence. These things, by their very nature, cannot be stable. Sometimes the soul grasps at one physical object, sometimes at another. There is no one single essential desire that can concentrate the animal soul in the same way that the Divine soul concentrates its desire on God.

We now turn to an examination of the soul in relation to the different "Worlds" according to the Kabbalah. It is said that the five levels of the soul parallel the four worlds or levels of universal existence: Action, Formation, Creation, Emanation. The animal soul relates primarily to the World of Action, the spirit to the World of Formation, and the Higher Soul (Neshamah) parallels the world of Creation. These are the levels that ordinary men reach, and beyond which only the chosen few can be said to penetrate. The level of Creature (Chayah) in the soul is contingent to the world of Emanation, and the level of Yechidah (Unity) in the soul is a merging of the soul in God. Such a state of unity in the soul goes beyond desire, for it has already realized itself; the entire soul is focused on one point, the Divine spark, a veritable part of the Divine reality. This unity in a person's soul is actually a point that includes all souls. That point of concentration of all the souls in one central unity is called "Knesset Yisrael." It is also known as Shechinah and as the Kingdom (Malchut) of God on earth, a coming together of all things. The animal soul, in contrast, has no such focus; the objects of its desires are dispersed.

We may note here that the image of the Divine soul as a

spark or as a flame is limited to its upward aspiration. When unity is reached, this image is no longer valid. The Divine soul may rather be likened to a burnt-out flame, the consummation of the fire. The soul, all eagerness toward God, rises as a flame until it reaches its higher source and merges with it. With unity, there is peace.

Two illustrations show the way in which each of the souls attaches itself to God: father–son, and teacher–pupil. The pupil does not bind himself to the very essence of the teacher. He relates primarily to the learning, wisdom, and the support coming from the teacher, and these may be diverse in their effects. In short, the connection is basically one of influence. The connection between father and son, on the other hand, is one in which the bond is immutably fixed by nature, not dependent on anything else. Nothing can change it; it is of the nature of "unity."

Thus the connection between father and son is single and indivisible, even though their outer relations vary with time. The relations between teacher and pupil, however, undergo alterations at the very core of their association and can even be severed, depending on the teacher's degree of influence. The connection of the Divine soul with God is more like that of father and son, changeless and constant, whereas the animal soul, being based on shifting preferences, can become any number of things, including a Divine soul. The Divine soul can never become an animal soul, focused as it is so completely on one point. To be sure, it can be in exile, but the basic relation to God cannot disappear. To maintain that, in purely spiritual terms, the father–son relationship is superior to the bond of teacher–pupil is not what one expects. But considering the fundamental essence of any bond, the father–son relationship may be lower in terms of give and take, but it is more fundamentally real for both of them because it is immutable and irretrievable.

The desires of the animal soul belong to the shell whose essence is that of taking and not giving. When we get to giving, to bearing fruit, we have holiness. As it is written in the *Zohar:* "The Sitra Achra is castrated and does not give fruit." That is, the evil cannot create anything, and if it does fashion something it does so by virtue of the powers of the good, the spark from the Divine it bears within itself and without which it could not exist.

We now come back to our beginning statement: "Draw me after thee and we will come running." The singular "me" pertains to the Divine soul, and the plural "we" relates to the many desires of the animal soul which give vitality to the being and will come running with the unity in order to "cling to Thee." This is the key to what a man wants. "Draw me" comes first, so that we may be able to run after the good in us.

The question of the very existence of the animal soul may be raised at this point. What is it and what is its nature? How shall we understand the intention behind the creation of the animal soul, with its compulsive pursuit of illusionary (external) satisfactions? The answer given is that without the animal soul, there would be no need for its opposite (as darkness arouses the need for light). The essence and meaning of life depend on a transformation of darkness to light, and this is nothing less than a miracle. A famous allegory helps to explain the creation of the world and the reason for the existence of the animal soul. In a royal palace there was a talking bird which was kept in a cage within the king's inner chamber. The ministers of the king came to him complaining, "Why do you take the talking bird into your inner chamber, when any small child can speak better than the bird?" The king answered: "True, even a child can talk better, but he belongs to the species that talks, whereas the bird is a creature that is not of this species and nevertheless talks; such a wondrous thing is worthy of occupying my inner chamber." This allegory explains the place of man in comparison with angels. This low-minded man-creature can reach a special status precisely because, in spite of his being earthbound and physical, he still can recognize God and "chirp" like a talking bird.

This is what awakens God's love for one. The world is altogether the play of God; but this is another side of the question. As the Chasidic master sees it, the transmutation of darkness into light is not merely a play. The light created from the darkness, the will issuing from the animal soul, is, in its essence, of a higher quality than what previously existed. So the light coming from the animal soul is not just an interesting phenomenon, it is the creation of something new and greater, without which the correction of evil could not take place.

10

The Many Sides of Chesed

E ven a Talmid Chacham (Scholar of the Torah) needs a certain increment of pride, no matter how small, in order to be creative. In the same way, a person who, out of an excess of humility, has crushed the power to create, cannot really achieve the level of a Talmid Chacham. This problem is indeed a very real one because there are many people who, upon reaching a certain level of self-renunciation and egolessness, could be creative in a significant manner but fail to be so because they feel they are too small. Some people need more self-confidence or pride, others require less, but a minimum is essential. What we are pointing to is the aspect of good within what is considered evil, and the evil that can issue from the most refined goodness.

A key to an understanding of this matter resides in the nature of Chesed, the Sefirah of Grace and Lovingkindness, the urge to give of oneself to others. At one extreme of this Attribute we have holiness, and at another we have a dangerous uncleanness such as that which occurs when the flow of grace gets out of control and exceeds the bounds of the permitted. In regard to love, for example, a person, whether man or woman, should love all men, but there is a limit that cannot be crossed with impunity. As was said of Ishmael, the symbol of the tendency to excess passion: from too much loving, all manner of iniquity can follow – fornication, violence, and even murder. In Kabbalistic terms it may be said to be a matter of learning the bounds of the vessel which contains or defines a certain Attribute. Grace is grace, strength is strength, joy is joy – each is an authentic and real quality in itself. But a quality is corrupted when it ceases to be aware of its limits. When joy gets out of bounds and becomes frivolous, it can begin to clown and mock and act the buffoon, at which stage it quickly takes on the nature of the Shell, the Klipah, and may be considered the Chesed of Philistinism. Philistinism is that which only imitates, having lost touch with the essential form or vessel that contains the Divine Attribute.

The Chesed of Ishmael is still Chesed, even though it has become a Shell. The Chesed of Philistinism, however, is no longer Chesed; it has become self-destructive. Anything that carries on unrestrainedly for its own sake tends to rush into the arms of the terrible.

In both cases, when there is an abundance of life, there is chance of restoration to the holiness of Chesed. But when there is a void or emptiness to begin with, correction is much more difficult. It quickly becomes something of another order, for the problem is the ability to express a certain content and not a lack of content.

Concerning this matter of content, the Baal HaTanya

classifies the different types of men. Some men are of the nature of sheep, others of the goat, and others like the ox. The sheep is an innocent animal and is easily led. There is something of holiness in its capacity for self-renunciation and its incapacity to do any harm. The goat is more lively and liable to cause trouble. The ox may actually be dangerous. On the other hand, when the ox is harnessed to the plow, it can be very useful. The sheep cannot draw the plow, but it can be offered up as a sacrifice. It has no inner force, and, alas, it is only force that can be harnessed. Some men may have an external show of force (like the goat), but it is only a show, and quite useless. Certain animals make sounds that are loud enough to be heard far away, even though they themselves are small and insignificant; the lion's roar, however, is an expression of real strength.

Obviously, then, there are many levels of Klipot. Philistinism, for example, is largely a matter of emptiness and good intentions. Its clutching at Chesed and holiness is not due to any real inwardness. Often there is no goodness at all to speak of; it is more like a farce. Indeed, there is no reason to believe that the prankster, the mountebank, for all his laughter, is a better person than anyone else. One may even be inclined to feel something suspect about the desire to make fun of others or enjoy situations for oneself.

On the other hand, Abraham, who is the chief representative of Chesed, said, "I am but dust and ashes" (Genesis 18:27). He thus nullifies himself as a meaningful reality. This self-renunciation seems like a contradiction to Chesed's lovingkindness, with its power of giving. After all, Chesed is an expansiveness of outward-going feeling, while nullification is a withdrawal and contraction inward. The aspect of Abraham as signified by water seems different from that of the Abraham of "dust and ashes." But perhaps this capacity to spread out in all directions, like water, is connected with the capacity to be as dust and ashes, which, being superfluous, also renounces definiteness. One who sees himself as being of no account and without importance can more easily give all that he is and all that he possesses to others.

There is also a giving that comes from a feeling of fullness and plenty, a sense of "greatness" in the positive sense of being beyond need.

Some people live in their own narrow world and are stingy to themselves. But they do so not out of miserliness, for there are people who can realize that other people are in need but fail to see that they themselves are no less in need. There is a story in the Midrash Rabbah about some scholars who came to a city to raise money for charity. They sent one of their number to observe the household of a certain illustrious citizen in order to ascertain how much to ask of him. The scholar came to the house and by chance over-heard the rich man scolding his wife, insisting that she buy a cheaper brand of lentils for their table. The scholars therefore did not even bother to approach him for money but collected their charity from others. When they were about to take their departure, the rich man complained to them, "Why didn't you come to me?" They explained the reason, and he answered, "Concerning that which belongs to me, I chose to be stingy, but about that which belongs to God I prefer to be generous."

Ultimately, however, real charity is not only a matter of regarding the needs of others, it is a matter of not seeing oneself. If one is truly nothing in his own eyes, one is able to offer up the plenitude of oneself without experiencing a sense of loss. There is no reckoning – this one should get so much, that one something else, and I too deserve something. When the giver is out of the picture, like dust and ashes, there is no one above or below him, there are no levels of value, and the act of giving is spontaneous, natural, and simple. Many of the greatest Sages of Israel used to be like that, charitable in this unthinking, uncalculating manner while being themselves unsure of their own worth, constantly in doubt about their spiritual progress. True charity makes the giver only a channel for transference of value, one who believes that everything should go to others and nothing is due him – like the Rabbi who could not fall asleep if there was any money in the house.

Such is the quality of true Chesed. So that the Patriarch Abraham, who is the counterpart of Chesed, is considered to be of the nature of the Chariot, a vehicle of expression for Divine grace. He was able to be such a one because of his capacity to nullify himself, to be like dust and ashes. For the principle of holiness is the elimination of feeling of the self, the ability to be a vessel for Divine love and fear. The more feeling of self, no matter of what kind it is, the more it becomes, inwardly at least, of the nature of the shell.

This leads us to consider a general principle concerning avodah zarah (idolatry). What are other gods? Are they not the result, at the other extreme, of the idea that there is something else besides the Holy One, Blessed be He? Of course, this is at the extreme end, while at close range, we have the miniature idolatry, when a person worships himself. To be sure, it depends on the situation; sometimes it is quite emphatically avodah zarah and there are people for whom the self is the only deity whose authority they are willing to accept. As the Sages have said, anyone who is proud is like one who worships idols, the common factor being the acknowledgment of one's self as primary. Also, a person who surrenders to anger or any passion is like one who indulges in a sacrificial rite to himself.

Recognizing this subtle relationship between idolatry and self-indulgence, the Rabbis used to impose elaborate penances as corrections (Tikun) for sin. An example was the case of an adulterous woman in France some two hundred years ago. The rabbi admitted that one could not be as harsh as in old times and he prescribed a penance of a year-long (daytime) fast, during which she was restricted to certain foods which were to be eaten only once a day on Sabbaths and on Feast days; after that year she was to continue fasting moderately (twice a week) for another three years; she was never to sleep on a bed, only on the ground, and so on and on. All this was in due consideration of the alleviating factors in the case and the rabbi's inclination toward leniency. The "corrections" or Tikunim imposed by the Ari are in the same vein; they include fasts of 184 days for a single eruption of anger, for anger is a form of avodah zarah and therefore a most grievous sin.

We are here repeating the well-known truth that whenever the self persists, God is not apparent. The other side of this truth is that the Divine grace emanates from above

126

incessantly and without limit because of its "unfathomable greatness." There is no end to the power of love; it penetrates to the farthest corner of existence. In this sense, we say that the man Abraham is a chariot of Divine Chesed. The Patriarchs can be viewed as chariots because they are at a level where they are wholly controlled, where they are like tools in the hand of God. In fact, whenever any human being can make himself wholly passive to the Divine, he becomes such a vehicle of a Divine attribute.

The Chesed of Ishmael is the very opposite of the Chesed of Abraham. It springs from a certain arrogance, a sense of one's own importance. The greater the person, the more emphatically is this kind of Chesed expressed. The goodness and generosity reflect the feeling of one's own worth, so that, for instance, it would be beneath one's dignity to bestow anything but the finest gifts and the most expensive gratuities. The quality of love is submerged by the quality of pride. To be sure, Chesed is still present – there is a genuine impulse to share one's being – but it can also be expressed in the extreme case of a tyrant boasting of the number of people he had killed. The self has expanded beyond its constraints; instead of self-nullification there is self-aggrandizement. The Chesed of Ishmael is not remotely similar to the Chesed of Abraham in spite of external resemblances, such as hospitality; the former is gracious only to show off one's munificence, the latter because of a love of the stranger.

The soul, being free, can express its uniqueness in any number of ways. But the Chesed of Ishmael abuses this freedom and is no longer a Divine Attribute; it has severed its connection with the Chesed that feels impelled to do good. For there is an aspect of giving that is built on the need of a person to give of himself whatever he feels that another should have. This is the genuine aspect of self-nullification and making oneself a channel for the transfer of grace, in contrast to the giving of that which is superfluous, of that which one no longer requires.

The difference between the two kinds of Chesed can become the test of the individual. The aspect of Abraham is to be as "dust and ashes." Ashes are remnants, that which is left over after something has been burnt or used up. One is in the position of saying: I am only the remnants of Chesed, the ashes of some burnt-out good. The Chesed of Ishmael, however, becomes an aspect of the superfluities of oneself. The difference between them is that Abraham sees himself as useless and sees others as principal, while Ishmael sees others as useless and gives them what is superfluous. And as is known, the haughty of this world like to throw their money around, not because they like to give it to others but because it is an expression of their "greatness." Often, what is a luxury for one may be a necessity for another, and no matter how welcome the gift of those who have too much, it can hardly be called Chesed. The Chesed of Abraham is associated with an impulse to giving all, including that which he himself needs. When a person gives all that is most precious to him, it is genuine giving; when a person gives what is of no importance to him, it is not giving at all.

This is true of other things as well, such as thoughts or feelings. Who is a hero? He who conquers his impulse. His own impulse, and not that of another, because there are

128

many varieties of impulse. One person is repelled by another's urgent impulse to play cards and carouse all night and has no trouble in relinquishing such temptations; another cannot conceive of devoting himself to only one woman and hasn't the slightest romantic impulse. It is easy enough to overcome a desire that is of no consequence to one's being. Giving is a matter of renouncing that which really matters.

It may be observed that both the Chesed of Ishmael and the Chesed of Philistinism are derived from the Chesed of Abraham, as a sort of remnant, as that which is discarded. The Chesed of the Philistines is only external, a parody of the Chesed of Abraham, and in many ways it is not Chesed at all. Although it draws upon certain external expressions of Chesed, like gladness, it subtly distorts the expression.

In other words, one can seriously copy, or pretend, or dress up in the garments of the genuine, and all too often the imitation is hard to distinguish. There are people for example, who use fine words to clothe their thoughts, and there are those who cling so tenaciously to their thoughts that they cannot find words for them, and another kind of distortion results. Thus, the smiles and laughter, the tone and the words of Chesed are easily imitated and frequently confused in numerous varieties of expression.

What is more, the garments themselves change, sometimes independently of what they are clothing. For instance, one can study Scripture for reasons other than love of Torah, such as pride or esthetic pleasure, and this can become a respected value. Fortunately, most such distortions have their correction built in. Sometimes the distortion

129

is difficult to discover and therefore not easy to correct. Nevertheless, it is recommended that a person should occupy himself with Torah and Mitzvot, even if not for their own sake, because eventually this would lead to doing it for their own sake.

The genuine alternative to the Chesed of Abraham is Gevurah, the aspect of Isaac. Rather than being outgoing and joyous, a matter largely of the heart, the aspect of Isaac, or Gevurah, is withdrawal inward, a concentration of strength and a sense of awe. It is connected with control and restriction, with the setting of specific limits and clear definitions. With Abraham, in contrast, there are hardly any limitations; all is open, free, and inviting, in relation to things, to people, and to God. Isaac, while establishing frontiers and feeling confident enough to judge the world, at the same time has the great-heartedness and the need for the expression of love. This expression, however, takes the form of another kind of nullification, a kind of retirement, if not actual seclusion, a fear of wrong action, a dread of doing something that may cause harm to someone else.

These two Attributes exist in varying degrees in people, and they cannot be contrasted as good and evil. For example: A pupil was asked why he prayed so fast. He answered that the prayer was so pleasant and sweet to him that he grabbed as much as he could. The rabbi said: Do you think that for me prayer is not pleasant? (The rabbi was known to spend more time in prayer than was usual.) The pupil replied that the rabbi's prayer is like burning coals, and such are not to be swallowed speedily. In other words, the matter can be viewed from different angles. There are people for

130

whom restrictions are not necessary; they have to be free to expand in all directions. But there are also those who require clearly defined controls. As the Rabbi of Kuritz, a great exponent of truth, once said: The difference between that fellow and myself is that he so much loves the truth that he speaks it constantly and sometimes a trifling untruth enters, whereas I so dread a lie that I hardly speak at all in order to avoid letting an untruth be uttered.

A similar relation may be said to prevail between Gevurah and Chesed. The attitude of fear of evil in the former restrains one's expression, makes one practice control and seek perfection in word and deed. The attitude of benevolence and fullness in the latter may induce spontaneity and joy. They are not contradictory; they are different aspects of Divine plenty and belong to different kinds of personality.

What is more, the Attribute of Gevurah may well be able to show more compassion and understanding than Chesed or Tiferet (Beauty, Harmony, Compassion). Since Gevurah begins from below and struggles upward to the light, since it knows the nether world of matter and sin more intimately than does Chesed, it is better able to empathize. Since Isaac, or Gevurah, is on the side of Tikun, his task is to make right that which goes wrong; Gevurah is thus a constant improvement, not only a bringing up from below but a raising of that which is in darkness to the light. Chesed begins from above, expands in every direction including below, and only by way of inclusiveness does it touch upon the little things, the insignificant and small in human life.

Isaac's name in Hebrew is Yitzchak, "he who will laugh." Since he is never reported to have laughed, his name seems to be a contradiction to his personality. But his name is directed to the future. It says that Gevurah, which is now severity, will some day rise up and become greater even than Chesed. Chesed is easy – for one who is all grace and love it is easy to be gracious and loving – but for Gevurah, who is awe and control and critical judgment, it is much more difficult, and so when it does happen, there will be laughter on earth as well as in heaven.

11

The Great Awe of
Pachad Yitzchak

The profound problems issuing from the Bible narrative of the Binding of Isaac revolve around the primary factor of "Pachad Yitchak." In Kabbalistic terms it is identified with, and goes beyond, the Sefirah of Gevurah (Severity), which is both Isaac and Fear, and is seen as an esoteric key to the reception of Divine Light. The greater the appearance of the Divine Light, that is, the closer one gets to it, the greater the annihilation and nullification of self, the greater the "Fear of God." Indeed, in this world it is almost impossible to experience the Divine Fear of God and the subsequent self-nullification (with all its splendor) because we are too far away from the source of the Light. We cannot get close enough to know this Divine Fear. In order to experience any emotion we have to be on an equal plane with the cause of the emotion, or at least not on such a distant or disproportionate plane that whatever seeks to influence us is far and away beyond our capacity to even be conscious of it. That is to say, there is no contact at all where the gap is excessive.

In the upper worlds, whenever a contact is made with a higher power that is too much for the creature, it is burned up, utterly consumed. In the lower worlds, as said, such a contact seldom if ever occurs. Only in the ultimate future, when there will be a far greater downpour of the power to bear the Divine Light, will the fear of God and the knowledge of His awesome glory be experienced. Now we do not really feel the fear of God, not because God is absent but because we are not on a sufficiently high plane to apprehend His presence.

It is therefore claimed by many that "Pachad Yitzchak," this true Divine awe or fear, cannot be known in the nether world of human affairs, it can be experienced only at the highest level, in the World of Atzilut (Emanation). The World of Emanation is that realm beyond all the knowable worlds of Briyah, Yetzirah, and Assiyah (Creation, Formation, and Action) and thus is almost impossible to talk about. To help us grasp a little of its meaning, it may be appropriate to dwell on the Tree of Life and the Tree of Knowledge of Good and Evil.

It is written: "And the Lord God planted a garden eastward (Kedem) in Eden. . . . the Tree of Life also in the midst of the garden, and the Tree of Knowledge of good and evil" (Genesis 2:8–9). Although the Hebrew word "Kedem" is usually translated "east," there are contexts in scriptural writings where the word signifies "before" in terms of time. In this case, the Garden was formed before the world was created, before time was. It therefore must be regarded as belonging to the World of Atzilut, from which everything emanated.

At the same time, according to the Kabbalah, the Garden of Eden is an aspect of the Sefirah of Malchut (Kingdom). In the esoteric tradition, the word "garden" also signifies the plane of holiness. Such is its meaning, for example, in the Song of Songs, where expressions such as "a garden enclosed" and "the garden of nuts" have special symbolic connotations.

The Tree of Life belongs entirely to the World of Atzilut which is absolute wholeness, while the Tree of Knowledge of Good and Evil points to the World of separation, to a breaking up into various entities which have lost their connection with one another. The Tree of Knowledge grows in the Garden, in the World of Atzilut, but its influence extends into the lower worlds of separation, Briyah (Creation), Yetzirah (Formation), and Assiyah (Action). That is, even those celestial worlds of Briyah and Yetzirah, which are so far above us, are still marked by division, even if so superior and sublime that we cannot be aware of it.

The principle of spiritual unity is expressed by the capacity for the same thing to be manifest in several forms and on a number of different planes. Even when there is a separation of aim and purpose, or a distinct difference of being on various planes of being, there is a certain mutuality of influence, each one amplifying or reacting to the other in hidden ways. Whereas in the worlds of separation there is an I, a You, and a He, each with its own identity. God is within, opposite, and outside.

Thus even the angel or the seraph, who belongs to the World of Briyah, is part of the scheme of separation, and

137

each has its own identity and function. Even though the angel is no more than a messenger, or in our own human terms, a will-less nonentity incapable of independent action. It does possess a separate and unique self, just as a domestic animal can be subservient to the will of a human master and yet remain a distinct creature having its own desires, habitual reactions, and so on. The horse is not the same as the rider even if it does only the will of the rider.

Still, the Divine Chariot, which is the symbol of the Shechinah, needs a driver. Or, to take another Biblical metaphor, the axe is in the hands of the woodcutter. In all these cases, the will of the master of all action is done and the instrument's own will merely chooses to comply as a passive tool.

The fact is that precisely because a creature does not possess a real self of its own – every "I" that it identifies with does the work of God – it does not have any creative power of its own. At best it can only unite with, or get caught up in, some other creaturely force. But through all the worlds of separation, the Tree of Knowledge extends as the source of all contrasts and judgment. Although the Tree of Life is also present, man is forbidden to eat of it lest he live forever. Adam was banished to the lower levels of being, out of the World of Emanation, which is entirely good, because he had become acquainted with evil. Even in the highest of the lower worlds, the world of Briyah, which is entirely pure, there are elements of differing aspects, connections, and interactions. This separation, or inclusion of separate entities, is already an intimation of good and evil, of an "I" of sorts and all that results from it; it is the beginning of the process that ends in death. Good and evil together can never belong to the scheme of eternal life.

In some midrash exegesis it is said that Adam at first reached from one end of the world to the other, but that after sinning, God put His hand on him and Adam's size was diminished to the human stature. The Kabbalah deals with the matter as a principle concerning the nature of man. A man should strive to penetrate beyond the fourth dimension of time into the fifth dimension of experience, where he reaches the other extreme of existence, original being. Instead, the range of human experience, the stature of man, extends only so far as his ego reaches.

At present, it may be said that there are persons who, spiritually at least, have less than a certain minimum of human stature and are therefore at a very low level, quite near to the dust of the ground. Nevertheless man remains a higher being in potential, a son of Adam, reaching out to the World of Atzilut. He is located in several places at once, in the various worlds of separation, his feet in one place and another part of him in the higher spheres, and he may never become aware of the higher worlds, especially the World of Atzilut. Nevertheless the Tree of Life remains a part of his life, just as the Tree of Knowledge does.

Thus in the Bible, Abraham binds Isaac to the (fire) wood on the altar ("wood" in Hebrew is "tree"), to the two trees of Life and Knowledge. He does so because in order for Isaac to reach the Tree of Life in Atzilut he has to be raised on the altar by the transformation called "Pachad Yitzchak," the terrible awe or fear of Isaac. According to the esoteric wisdom, Abraham raises Isaac above the wood (trees) on the altar, above the earthly, to a level that enables him to stretch to his full stature, the stature of Isaac, which is Pachad Yitzchak, which is Gevurah in the chart of the Holy Sefirot.

In the lower world, Isaac could not be revealed as such. It is a world too covered over and separate, too much divided, dense and incapable of receiving the light of revelation. In this world Isaac remains well hidden, visible in terms of Severity, and only in the higher levels does he emerge in his true glory and greatness as Divine Awe and Fear.

It becomes possible when Abraham (Chesed) raises him, as only the Divine Love which is Chesed can do. For Isaac cannot remain forever below. He has to be elevated to a higher plane, and this is achieved only if he is somehow merged with Chesed (Love), which is Abraham. Alone he cannot do it, even though he may attain a kind of power and greatness of his own.

This merging of Chesed and Gevurah comes about as an act of sacrifice on the part of Abraham. It is an inner sacrifice, because the relations between Abraham and Isaac are very complex, a mixture of many subtle and strong forces. Neither can continue far in a straight line, because of built-in obstacles. There are gradations and levels of integration such as the Gevurah of Chesed and the Chesed of Gevurah. And of course they are dependent on one another.

"Without wisdom there can be no fear (awe), without fear there can be no wisdom" (Sayings of the Fathers, Ch. 3). The question of which comes first or is paramount has no simple answer. We have the same problem of levels and gradations: A certain level of fear is not attained except by wisdom, since one has to realize the fearfulness of something before being afraid of it; and also a certain awe, a combination of wonder and dread, accompanies the growth of wisdom. There is an undefinable inner order, an unchartable progress, in their mutual development. This may be sensed in the way the expression concerning the union of fear and love can be switched from union in fear and love (יחוד בדחילו ורחימו) to the union in love and fear (רחימו ודחילו). In each case the order is charged with spiritual meaning.

To be sure, these matters are dealt with at great length by the Sages. Here all we can do is mention the result of much deliberation. Thus, there are two levels of "fear" of God. One is called יראה חטאה, lower fear, which is also dread; the other is יראה עילאה, higher fear which is awe and shyness, in the sense of being responsive to the sublimity of the Light. The higher fear, that of awe, is a requisite for love. Without it, there is no real love. To be sure, there are vast differences in the scale of values, in the emotional patterns, between one generation and the next, but within this constant change of style, this relation of love to fear varies only externally.

The generally accepted order in the social world is that fear should come first, in the form of assumption of responsibility. The voluntary shouldering of obligation or a yoke of some sort is the simplest expression of the fear of God. It connotes that the doing, the fulfilling of the Divine command, is a proof of faith, to be followed by the act of listening, which is also the readiness to understand. As the children of Israel called out, "We shall do and we shall hear," נעשה ונשמע. Only after the act of obedience comes the experience of comprehension. By bending the will to see certain truths, love is granted. According to this order, fear comes first, followed by the understanding in which a person becomes a receptacle able to receive love.

Of course, there are many aspects to this simple order. One of the difficulties is that for every kind of love, no matter on what level, there has to be an object of love. This can become quite problematic, as in the case of Ishmael, son of Abraham. He inherited so much of the capacity for love, yet he misdirected it to self-indulgence and fornication, a kind of refracted light, making oneself the object of love in terms of the pleasure it gives. It is a loving oneself through another object or person. The "other" becomes a means of expressing self-love. Even language has no qualms about saying of someone that he "loves" fish for dinner.

This suggests a very wide range of gradations and levels of love. Indeed what is often called love can be something entirely different. The feeling can get so entangled in the dark web of personality that what emerges is of a very different essence. When love draws mainly from the outside for its sustenance and not from the inner resources, when it seeks to receive and not to give, demanding and not easily accepting, it becomes something else, a negative force. Whether it be the relations between man and woman, parents and children, person and person, or group, in order for love to be "true," the self has to be diminished and not augmented. The ultimate test of love is the degree of nullification of the "I" and the amount of space thereby provided for the other. Love is thus seen as a dynamic relation, based on the thoughts of others and not on the thoughts of oneself.

This need to eliminate the pre-eminence of the self in order to relate properly to another now seems fairly self-evident, but it was through the Binding of Isaac and Isaac's Fear that this self-nullifying love was deeply incised into the consciousness of the race. Because love and passion are so intensely intertwined, the self has to become properly attuned to receptivity in order to avoid losing all; that is, it must become a suitable vessel for the love of God. This receptivity is a readiness to receive something that one cannot know or anticipate and to be its instrument.

We have said that the higher level of Fear called supreme awe, יראה עילאה, expresses the Fear of God that precedes Love, which is expressed by total acceptance. Higher fear is accompanied by a genuine humility; altogether it is a very complex integration of connections with God. It leads to many levels of experience and perceptions bringing about a certain understanding of the nature of the higher worlds. There is a story of a peasant who, on meeting the king in the fields without knowing who he was, offended the royal majesty. The courtiers wished to take the peasant's life, but the king suggested an even more severe punishment: to bring the poor wretch to court and let him learn the enormity of his transgression. In order to attain an adequate grasp of the higher fear, one has to learn to recognize how little one understood previously. This suggests that there are also disadvantages to knowledge of the higher fear; life is much simpler without it.

Where there are no problems, no "fear," it is because there was no connection. Obviously, where there is no contact, one cannot feel much of anything, certainly not awe or fear. At best, one can warn the ignorant a little, prepare them by

143

a minimal education to be able to receive the wonder of the contact when it comes without spoiling it for themselves.

The first thing, then, is not to spoil an experience by rejection or resistance; one has simply to accept it and enter into some meaningful relation with it. After an effort to understand even if only a little, it is possible to reach a level of higher fear, of awe or a subjective response to the sublime.

What is being explained here is that in order for Isaac, the sacrifice, to become "Pachad Yitzchak" or Gevurah (Strength), he has to reach this higher level of Fear and he can do so only through Abraham, the higher Love which is Chesed. The problem is one of distance. One can easily get stuck in the lower Fear, unable to get out of it, and suffer all that this implies. In order to pass on and to overcome the great distance to the higher Fear, one has to rise in a number of stages, through the levels of Love and gradations of Fear until that higher Fear becomes manifested. And at the very highest level of such Fear, one is also beyond Love itself.

But for Isaac to be elevated entirely above the wood (trees) on the altar, he has to merge into the Chesed of Abraham. Thus absorbed (and annihilated) in Love, the rite of the Binding of Isaac achieves its purpose. As it is said, Abraham bound Isaac hand and foot. What is the meaning of being bound hand and foot? It is a situation in which one is unable to act, to express or to be oneself; one is given over, subordinate, to another; one transcends the levels of fear until one becomes like a thing, without will, or at least the instrument of a higher will. In the Kabbalah, this is the nullification of the Sefirah of Kingdom (Malchut); becoming no more than a point under the Sefirah of Foundation (Yesod), one can rise ever higher up the Tree of Life.

144

A symbolic version of this process in the dynamics of Divine Fear is the ritual of the blowing of the shofar (ram's horn) at the New Year. There are three very specific chords: a soft, broken sound, which is the aspect of Chesed; a loud blast, which is the aspect of awe, "Yirah"; and a series of blasts, which is the combination of the other two chords. The tonal and rhythmic combinations should be sounded by someone who knows the Kabbalistic connotations and can reach a dramatic synthesis.

This synthesis is expressed by Jacob, the son of Isaac, who represents the middle line in the Tree of the Sefirot. He is part of the central pillar which extends from the "Crown" of the Tree to the other end which is the "Kingdom" of this world. He blends the right-hand line of Chesed with the left hand-line of Gevurah into the central Sefirah of Tiferet (Splendor, Compassion). In this way he is the ultimate outcome of the Binding of Isaac.

To be sure, this is not a simple synthesis: the central line emerges from the World of Atzilut (Emanation), branches off into the right-hand aspect of God as the Father and as Chochmah (Wisdom), and branches into the left-hand aspect of the Mother and of Binah (Understanding). The line of derivation from Chochmah and Binah is thus not a compromise between contradictory forces; rather it organically integrates all the aspects of the Tree of the Sefirot.

Two opposing elements can be brought closer together perhaps, but it is impossible to combine them and to integrate them without the intervention of a force above and beyond each of them. Here the integration of Chesed and Gevurah into a higher entity, a completely new essence, is possible because the force that makes it happen comes down from Keter and ultimately emanates from the World of Atzilut. (In a certain sense all sacrifice, like that at the Holy Temple, is a ritualistic expression of this process.)

A practical aspect of this fundamental relation stems from the identification of the right-hand line (Chesed) with Ge-milut Chasadim (Charity), the left-hand line (Gevurah) with Mitzvot (good works expressing the fulfilling of religious duties), and the middle line (Tiferet) with Torah (Study of Scripture): תורה, עבודה, גמילות חסדים. Of course, every mitzvah is based on the consecration of one's actions; it is a doing that adds something to the world. Thus, on one hand, the mitzvot can be seen as the performance of Chesed (Loving-kindess) at all levels and therefore not disconnected from charity. On the other hand, the left side of work (worship), whether sacrifice or prayer, is connected with Gevurah in terms of the act of releasing things from their covering, letting the potential come out and be expressed. At the same time, in the act of performing the mitzvah, one is also burning it up, consuming it by offering it up. Prayer for example, as worship (עבודה), is an endeavor to unite with God, which necessitates a removal from the sense of "I" and mine and involves a kind of elimination of the self within the framework of an aspiration to achieve a higher experience of being. Prayer at a certain level tends to become an act of self-destruction, a nullification of the self.

The middle line of Tiferet, also called Torah, is rooted in the relation to the other two, Charity and Work. These actually define the Study of Torah, extricating it from its apparent abstraction. For in Torah study one is forced to concentrate on, and to cling to, certain spiritual realities so

146

that a certain self-nullification takes place, and one also brings these same spiritual realities down to oneself, lowers them to the level of utility and action.

In this sense of a double connection, Torah study is not like any other mitzvah. I am within the subject and the subject is included within me. The essence of other mitzvot is that I take something that is profane, I add something to it, and I thereby convert it into something holy. In Divine worship (prayer) I do nothing of the sort. When I offer up something, I do in a sense hallow it by sacrificing it, but I am not adding anything to it. I am simply burning up the reality of its existence. That is, I am not making it higher than it was; I am annihilating it.

As for Torah, I do not raise the Torah that I study nor can I make it less than it is. In fact, it is only when I study (or obey) Torah that I raise my own soul. Also I create Torah when I relate to it. At the same time, I destroy (offer up) something of myself and the Torah gives something of itself to me. The relationship is the central line of the Sefirot, including as it does the highest extreme of Being and Knowledge and the lower extreme of this world.

The objects to which Torah directs us thus extend from one end of the universe to the other, from the edifying "Know the God of thy fathers" to the injunction to wash the hands before morning prayers. Both these are Torah and there is no contradiction; the main direction is basically vertical, upward, and downward: I in my place, try to raise myself out of the trivial to the great. First I try (the way of Chesed) to use prayer to forget the problems of daily life. In the ardor of worship, I seek to burn out the ordinary, to

147

extricate myself from the tangle of the insignificant detail and the trite. They cease to count so much. Then in performing the mitzvah (the way of Gevurah) I do the opposite: I take something of the Divine holiness and inject it into the trivial. While in Torah (the way of Tiferet), I do both at the same time; they are merged in a unified act. For Torah contains both Love and Fear, the right and the left side together. When a person does a mitzvah, he does not necessarily add anything to himself, but when a person studies Torah, he does acquire something.

Also when one prays one does not necessarily acquire anything. On the contrary, it is said that a person should not even enjoy it. If he gets pleasure out of prayer, out of seeing himself in the act of prayer, he should perhaps do something else. A Tzadik once went to an extreme in this respect—saying that he preferred someone who *said* that he fasted from one Sabbath to the next to someone who actually fasted, because a person who claims to fast deceives only others whereas a person who actually fasts deceives himself. So long as there is a feeling of triumph or satisfaction, the point is missed. What should remain has to be more in the nature of burnt ashes, or, at the highest level, no residue at all. The peak experience should be beyond all feeling, or the capacity to talk about it.

It is also maintained that the highest level of prayer cannot be visible from the outside. When someone is visibly devout in prayer, the prayer is likely to fall short of the highest. It was said of a certain Tzadik that when he prayed he looked like a burnt-out wick. He was nonexistent.

So while one is studying Torah, he is nullified by it at the same time that he is absorbing it. It can be said of many that there is a progression, that one enters ever more deeply into Torah and that one is also always being filled by the Torah that one is studying.

Let us now return to "Pachad Yitzchak," the core level of self-nullification, the result of the uncompromising confrontation of Abraham (Chesed) with Isaac (Gevurah). It is the highest point of Fear that can be reached, where it is no longer fear but a matter of facing the magnificence of His Glory.

Getting to know the fear of God involves many gradations. Some try to hide themselves from Divine punishment, for they see only the ferocity of inevitable retribution for sin. Such terror can take extreme forms. Others, like Job, are able to stand up to God, argue with Him about His seeming unfairness. There is also the terrible awe, which, as mentioned, is evinced as an extreme "shyness," a profound hesitancy or humility before the sublime, when persons hide themselves, not out of physical dread, but from a sense of being devastated by a greatness they cannot cope with. It is the fundamental fear of all finite creatures before the Supreme.

This hints at a region (or situation) that is above the Tree of Knowledge and the Tree of Life – beyond revelation itself. In the Book of Ezekiel there is a baffling description of the Celestial Creatures and the great Terror, of the terrible ice that is above the wings of the celestial creatures, the ice above the heavens, beyond all that is accessible to created things. Even if one of the Creatures themselves were to touch it, they would be utterly consumed, burnt up; which is why, as it is said, some of the higher angels are called Seraphs ("to burn") because that particular kind of celestial being is always burning.

In our world, the presence of evil makes it impossible for the "vessels" to grow without limit. All things must perish. Hence the need for "Pachad Yitzchak," to provide a means of breaking through the barrier. It is a matter of "returning" Light in the sense of the primordial Light. For in the very original beginning, it was Gevurah that expressed the source Light of Creation, but this could not last and all now functions differently. But when the world completes its present cycle and reaches the level of perfection, it will be able to accept this primordial true relation which will usher in the reign of the revelation of the Attribute of Gevurah. As it has been said, there is דחילו ורחימו and there is רחימו ודחילו. Terrible awe may, and sometimes must, precede and provoke the supreme love.

12

The Power To
Accept

It has taken 3,000 years to teach the Jews to keep the Sabbath with joy, as "Oneg Shabbat," delight of the Sabbath. To tell the people to refrain from doing any work on the seventh day did not require too much urging or educating, but to make the Sabbath day a sacrament and a joy is far more difficult. It takes ages because most of what has been learned over a long period of time can be destroyed in a single generation, and a new start has to be made. That this is still true today is evidenced by the behavior of certain hooligans in the religious quarter of Jerusalem who throw stones at other people who also do not have any idea of what the Sabbath means.

There seems to be a serious obstacle to a genuine acceptance of the Sabbath. The source of the difficulty may lie in the esoteric truth of the Sabbath, the fact that its light is a "returning" light, as the ancient wisdom calls it. The Sabbath does not take part in creation. During the week, one is active, doing things and working; on the Sabbath everything is simply put back in place, returned to their source.

The day of rest is the time for restoration to origin. In this respect, the ability to carry out the Sabbath is another sort of functional capacity than what is required in the days of the week; one is in another world, another life style. It is a totally different framework, wherein a person is able to remain passive within a very precise setting. One is empowered with a capacity to receive and to be free from the need to be active and to be always doing. Such an ease of being is a talent or competence, a quality in itself.

The power of receptivity or passivity is associated with the most fundamental of human relationships, that between man and woman, between Abraham and Isaac, between Chesed and Gevurah.

There is an old saying that "Greater is the promise of God to women than to men in the time to come" (Berachot 17a). That is, the male is not the permanently dominant element in this world, the element that actively paves the way for dynamic processes to take place. The opposite may also be true; the important element may be the receptive, who would rather restore things and keep them still than create and struggle. The passive expresses a need to serve and contemplate the world rather than to create new forms and build additional structures, a need to refine what has already been received and to give it added value, raise it up, before returning it.

The receptive thus characterizes a mode of being that is alien to the realistic approach of people in this world who seek to have some advantage. Indeed, the passive ones are pushed aside and sometimes thrust into an inferior position.

The problem is far more profound than any easy correspondence to male and female. We are all children of Abraham and Isaac and we try to imitate them. Nevertheless, at the end of days, when we are restored to our fathers, it is Isaac who will be paramount. He is the hidden patriarch, the passive one who is sacrificed, but he is the one who provides us with the strength to rise ever higher. The power he represents covertly, in his hiddenness, is the power that will enable the whole world to be redeemed.

We are thus led to the essential theme of our discussion, the aspect of Gevurah. According to the chart of the Sefirot, Gevurah is strength and severity, withdrawal and concealment, acceptance and resignation. Another name for this Sefirah is "Pachad Yitchak" (Isaac's Fear), which also represents the inclination to passivity – a desire to avoid reacting, to go inward, to dig wells and to draw forth living waters, not to wander in search of anything new.

Isaac himself, as Gevurah, thus symbolizes the return movement, likened to the eventual reversal of priority of the Levites over the Priests, of Beit Shammai over Beit Hillel, the Halachah of Rabbi Eliezer over that of Rabbi Yehoshua. That is, at the time of redemption, the left line of Gevurah, which is basically the line of passivity, will become the central line which is now dominated by the right line of Chesed, of giving, of influencing the world from above. When this reversal takes place, as part of the restoration of man to original perfection, the line of receptivity will become the channel of dispensation. In particular, the direction of the line of Gevurah will be transformed from "Dechilu Verechimu" (Fear and Love) to "Rechimu VeDechilu" (Love and Fear). The end of this process is Pachad Yitzchak, because Isaac was raised beyond fear into the awe of wonder and humility, which is the state ushering in the Messianic period.

Another facet of Gevurah is that of the feminine, as opposed to the masculine facet of Chesed. Here one has to remember that in Kabbalah we cannot apply the same rigidity of thought as in biology. What is of value for our purpose is the fact that the relationship between male and female is one of the most rudimentary ones in an extremely complex system of relations, human and otherwise. It is human and beyond the human also in the way we divide the lines of the Sefirot into masculine and feminine forces, as influencing factors and those receiving influence, as right and left.

It is interesting that in this framework of Jewish writings, woman, the feminine aspect, belongs to Gevurah (Strength) and man belongs to Chesed (Love). Gevurah, which is also severity and justice, seems to be the essential quality of the woman, whereas Grace and Mercy, the so-called soft-hearted aspect of human character, is considered essentially masculine. This seeming paradox is resolved by the idea that women are more sensitive but not necessarily more compassionate. There is a difference between sensitivity and compassion, between delicacy of perception and kind-ness of heart (chesed). Grace or Chesed is a definite At-tribute, whereas sensitivity is something else; it is a capacity that is not connected to any particular attribute or quality structure. People can be sensitive in terms of any trait or tendency within the framework of the intrinsic quality of their souls. They can be more or less sensitive in their expressions of Chesed or Gevurah. Persons who are easily stirred emotionally, whose enthusiasms are rapidly kindled or who are quick to fall in love, are sensitive. That is, they have a delicate reaction system, a more sensitive physical-nervous system. This does not belong to an inner soul quality, which remains the same whether sensitive or not. And, of course, the matter of men and women is not the important thing here. The essential principle is that the relation between Chesed and Gevurah is a relation between that which gives influence and that which receives influence. Only in this way is it considered a male–female relationship.

We are thus examining the feminine aspect of the Patriarchs. Isaac or Gevurah, is the receiver of the influence of Chesed and is therefore the feminine principle. People and things act upon him; he himself does not act. He does not go to get himself a woman; his wife is brought to him and she remains his only wife. But even if he is hidden and receiving, there is something attractive and powerful in his personality, a mystery of unprobed potential and new possibilities.

Everything about Gevurah, however, depends on the relation with the masculine principle of Chesed. One cannot conceive of any fulfillment of one without the other; there is no creative expression of Chesed without Gevurah, nor of Gevurah without Chesed. In life itself they have to be together, to function in some sort of harmony; otherwise there is chaos. Each one alone leads to disaster. The whole world of Tikun is built on the proper merging of these Sefirot.

157

Indeed, Tikun is possible only after absolute purity of concepts is renounced. Creativity requires a merging of qualities. Abraham and Isaac are not of different realms or character structures; they are two polar extremes, giving and receiving, and the relation between them is complex. Ultimately it is the passive that brings forth the fruit after being fertilized with its opposite.

There is a similar relationship between heaven and earth. In ancient times, the relation of heaven and earth was that of male and female, with the earth being mother and the sky being father to all that lives. The earth is unable to bear fruit without the rain from heaven.

As with the paradox of Isaac, the earth, the silent and receptive one, contains in itself the seed for all that will take shape. On the other hand, there is the matter of "feminine waters" (Mayim Nukvin), another cosmic aspect of the constant process of creation. As it is written in a certain introduction to the performance of mitzvot: In order for life to be meaningful, specific actions (mitzvot) have to be done to raise the feminine waters. This image, at its source, refers to the relation between God and the world. Rain and snow descend from the heavens to fructify the earth, as the words of God issue from the Divine source and animate life on earth. The earth can be seen to represent the lower world, which is the "Shechinah." Thus the creative relation between heaven and earth is conveyed by means of the higher waters which is the rain and the lower waters which is the subterranean waters. These latter may also be called "feminine" waters.

In the Talmud, which often moves easily from the most

sublime to the most earthly and parochial and back again, a passage in the Tractate Taanit says that the upper waters will not descend from above even a "tefach" (a handbreadth) until the lower waters rise toward them two tefachs. Elsewhere, the question is put: Why do we pray for rain? The answer includes many descriptive images, such as the groom going forth to meet his bride, and the drops of water in pools splashing up eagerly toward the rain that falls into the pool. The upper waters and the lower waters are attracted to each other, and the upper waters descend because the lower waters rise up toward them.

Genesis introduces this same image in the creation of a firmament to divide the waters above and the waters below and become a barrier between them. It is said that the lower waters, wishing to be before the King of the Universe, weep and complain: Why do we have to remain below and not above? Separation is suffering. One of the presumed answers of God to this separation is the salt of the sacrifice at the Holy Temple. Salt on the offerings on the alter represents the lower waters that want to rise up. There is a description of this in the answer to a Talmudic question: When are the days of joy greatest? When water is poured on the altar on the last day of Succot to bring the winter rains. The lower waters are offered up to fulfill themselves in joyful rising. When not offered up, the lower waters are considered weeping waters. The universal process is the essential relation between the one who receives influence and the one who influences.

An identical principle is evident in the interaction between direct Light (symbolized by Abraham) and returning or reflected Light (Isaac). They both serve the purpose of raising the lower, feminine waters. Another allegoric symbol is the emission of a woman's seed in order for the sperm to fertilize it. Still another image is the saying: On that day will living waters come forth from Jerusalem.

Isaac digs the wells through which the waters are brought up from the depths. His whole being is a movement from below upwards. His nature is to overturn the order of the world, for the world functions by virtue of forces flowing from above downward.

Thus the downpouring of Divine plenty is charted by the Kabbalistic tree in terms of Father–Mother, Chochmah–Binah, Upper–Lower Waters, and other forms of the Giver–Receiver pattern. It is a built-in aspect of all the worlds, and appears in each in different dimensions, on a variety of levels. There is a profound esoteric principle manifested in this view of influence force as a relation and not as a cause-and-effect phenomenon. It is very different from the mechanical grasp of natural law as a matter of action and reaction, and provides us with a truer and more compounded understanding of that which we explain by over-simplistic cause and effect reasoning. Altogether, then, the many-sided Kabbalistic concept of giving and receiving is thus also a way of understanding the creative process of Divine Light as it emanates forth, is reflected, and is absorbed.

In other words, the fundamental dynamics of life and existence, according to the Kabbalah, is not a simple straight line process, either horizontal or from above to below. There is a complex interrelationship of actions and reactions, multiple influences and contextual forces which operate on a number of dimensions and levels. Essentially it is a mutuality of influence, hardly ever a one-way cause and effect and, as said, it is not confined to the human, or even the biological spheres; it is a cosmic way. There is no rising of the feminine waters of Isaac (Malchut, or Earth) except they be "drawn" by the upper waters of Abraham. And vice versa.

The thinking here points to a conception that overturns the thermodynamic law of entropy, claiming as it does that there isn't just a one-way inevitable cooling influence of the active on the passive, but that the passive, in reacting, creates new situations. Abraham did not give birth to Isaac, he enabled him to be born; he acted on the feminine passive and thereby provided the possibility for Isaac to come into the world. Isaac's soul took advantage of the opportunity and came into the world to express that which was Isaac.

To go a little further into the mystery of birth, let us say that the body of the child is formed from the cells of the father and mother. The soul of the child, however, is formed by neither, but rather is created by a "copulation" of the Sefirot. When the Sefirot mix with one another, they give birth to souls and these souls are combinations of Sefirot in an infinite variety of relations. Every time and in every place where there is a new combination (usually the combinations are old, fairly fixed), a new soul is born. A new formation results, for example, from a certain selection or a distinguishing process. This birth is Chochmah speaking directly (for although wisdom is the creative power, it rarely expresses itself except through the other Sefirot).

The Kabbalah is full of stories about the birth of souls,

with keen insights into the period of the fetus and of suckling, the need for a proper weaning and eventual growth into independence of thought and will. There is a first growth and a second growth, with definite stages. Most of the stages of growth of the physical organs are accomplished in concealment (before the development of consciousness), while the stages of growth of the soul, in its larger scope, are accomplished as adults. That is, the soul in the adult must go through its own stages of embryonic growth and suckling, then by the mental development, first of the smaller mind and then of the larger mind. There are Kabbalistic works that see this growth in specific stages as a cosmic principle. They give detailed accounts of the growth of the year, its cycles and seasons, days move through embryonic periods, suckling, and stage after stage of development.

It is said, the soul of Elijah the prophet grew a twelve-month, and thereby absorbed the turgid waters that have to made clear, for a human embryo can linger and not be born in its given time. Such a soul is a strange soul and is likened to Elijah, who spoke of himself as a soul lingering before God. This lingering, or remaining still, is the characteristic of the angel, who stands before God, while man walks before God. Man cannot be standing; if he does, he is either an inanimate object or an angel. The angel stands–he cannot grow and must remain fixed and unchanging before the Divine. According to the Sages, since man can grow and change, he has a certain advantage over the angel.

Elijah said, "As the Lord God of Israel lives before whom I stand" (I Kings 17:1). This statement raises the possibility of Elijah's being an angel rather than a whole human being. Furthermore, Elijah himself declares that he is too much for the world. His soul is too big for the essence of things below and cannot quite arrange itself here, so it is sent forth, expelled so to speak, to another dimension, to angelhood. That is, it is a soul at a higher level, composed of the stuff of angels, having grown beyond its human measure, having gone beyond the cycles and crises of life.

The process of birth, with all its uncleanness, is itself considered a crisis, possibly the first in a long series of "severities" (Gevurot) to be experienced. It is in the nature of the fetus not to continue its fantastic growth in the womb but to be cast forth into the world. The child's growth then has to continue in a different framework. He has to pass through the ordeal of weaning, which is the cessation of being fed, and he has to keep moving on to phase after phase. If a child ever gets stuck at any particular stage, he becomes something else; there can be no lingering.

This, in a way, is the pattern of Creation. It must take its own course; the active dimension influences and determines the reality of the worlds and even constitutes their development through all the stages. The primary act of giving, the Light, does not vanish from the scene; it continues in one fashion or another, changing and forming and directing the growth of the receiver of influence. But it is also a circle that closes at some point. The feminine waters below reach a stage of clarity and a "woman of valor" arises. She becomes the housewife, in control of existence, above and beyond the husband. Such is the fertile relation of the creative process. Keter (Crown), the highest Sefirah, continues its active role, enabling all the Attributes to function and permitting Malchut (Kingdom) to grow. Malchut develops to the point where it no longer needs to receive influence and it becomes able to exert power, at which point it becomes Keter. There is a constant transformation, the lowest becoming the highest and the highest being transposed back into the beginning. In human life this process is translated as the mutuality of giving and receiving. In the chart of the Sefirot it is seen as the dynamics of the right (Chesed) and the left (Gevurah), and of the Upper (Keter) and the Lower (Malchut) realms.

Let us take, as an example, the flow of life from thought (the intention) to action (the end of the matter). Malchut, or Speech, is the vehicle of this process; it is the conscious aspect connecting the first impulse and the fulfillment of the action. The intention and the end of the matter are not always identical but they are certainly connected. What is more, there is a cycle: the end of the matter, the action, becomes intention at another level. Just as when one wishes to live in a house, there is a definite process that has to be followed. First is the conception of what is desired: how the house will look, how it should be constructed, the materials, and the labor. Then is the actual building, with its practical complexity and necessary adjustments. Finally is the moment of entering the house to live in it. In a way, this last step is the least creative part, and yet this end of the matter is the closing of the circle, the point of it all. The original intention meets itself. What was Keter has become Malchut and Malchut becomes Keter.

Thus the end of the matter and its beginning in desire are

to be seen as the two poles of the same unit of reality. But because the world is not perfect, or complete, the relation between Keter and Malchut is incomplete and imperfect. We are aware that there is much waste, there are any number of faults and defects in the process between wish and fulfillment. Much is lost.

This loss is not a part of the creative process itself; it is the result of friction, the faultiness of structure. Even if they are only external, the imperfections of the world make all relations suffer these effects of friction. The end of the matter, the final product, is seldom a precise copy of what was conceived in thought. But the essence of the creative process is such that sometimes, and not all that infrequently, the end of the matter is better, a more correct and more beautiful result than the one that had been intended. This is a mark of the basic wonder of creation. Indeed, whenever reality is more finely and more correctly integrated, then this extraordinary wonder strikes home – the world becomes more clear, transparent, and colorful, the relation between Keter and Malchut becomes a truly miraculous union.

Similarly, the relations among the other Sefirot – Chochmah, Binah, and Daat; Chesed, Gevurah, and Tiferet; Netzach, Hod, and Yesod – are often manifested in ways that are very trying for man. The emotions that we experience are usually far from the original beautiful and pure form of these emotions. Again, it is the faultiness of the world that makes it almost impossible for dream of reality to coincide with reality.

We are only too well aware of the common phenomenon

of the inadequacy of speech to express the thought behind it. One is made aware of difficulties, barriers, and obstructions along the way. On the other hand, when the obstructions are removed, when certain defects are overcome, the speech at the end of the matter can be richer and more eloquent than was anticipated. There can be an unexpected enhancement; words can be so full of emotional power and precision that they are, in turn, creative factors in the wheel of Malchut and Keter.

The fact that this does not happen all the time is due to the wasting of direct light in the world, the failure of the world to reflect the primal Light. Because we are not like mirrors in our reception of the light, because we are distorted in our being, wrong and greedy in our receiving, we are unable to benefit from the abundance of Divine Grace showered upon us. But when we can remove the faults and repair the defects, Malchut rises as high as Tiferet (Beauty). As it is written: "On that day living waters shall come forth from Jerusalem" (Zechariah 14:8). Jerusalem is Malchut.

13

Returning Light and Divine Laughter

It is written in the Scriptures that "Thou art our father though Abraham be ignorant of us and Israel acknowledges us not" (Isaiah 63:16). The Sages in Tractate Shabbat explained that this refers to our father Isaac, who will be the one to plead for us at the end of days. What is puzzling about this statement is the unquestioned fact that all three Patriarchs, Abraham, Isaac and Jacob, are our fathers. There must be some special meaning behind it, then, connected with the esoteric view of the End of Days, at which ultimate in time, Isaac, who corresponds to Gevurah (Strength) in the chart of the Sefirot, will be a more decisive factor than Chesed, which is Abraham (Divine Love or Grace), or Tiferet, which is Jacob (Divine Splendor, Harmony, Compassion).

Ordinarily, Isaac is below Abraham in the Kabbalistic order of things, and Jacob is the progenitor of the Children of Israel. What, then, is the origin of this strange notion that Isaac will be greater than the others?

Isaac, as Gevurah, represents both strength and control

(contraction). The essence of this Sefirah is a withdrawal inward that reflects a power of containment and of setting limits. At the same time, however, Gevurah is distinguished as the "returning light" radiating from below upward.

Chesed and Gevurah are the two main Sefirot among the seven lower Sefirot defining the human soul. We have already seen that Chesed is outward-going, a giving action, characteristic of the right line of the chart of Sefirot, symbolizing the direct Light pouring down from on high. The left line, dominated by Gevurah, symbolizes the Light being returned upward. They are like the movements of falling water versus blazing fire. Although there are a multitude of gradations of direct and reflected Light, essentially direct Light descends from a higher source to the receiver, and the reflected Light is the receiver's desire to rise toward or to give back to the giver. This latter movement (of Gevurah) thus has something of Chesed in it, in the sense that something is added to the giver.

On the other hand, Gevurah may be seen as a self-removal and an ascending leavetaking. From this point of view, Gevurah is no longer contraction, which is the action of that which wants to be present here, but rather the action of that which wants to leave and rise upward. Hence its representation as fire. The more intensely it burns, the more quickly it annihilates the reality, the lower substance of being, and rises to a higher substantiality. Therefore, too, it has more of the nature of a destructive force and, indeed, the relation to Gevurah has tended to be one of suspicion and fear. We are inclined to yearn longingly for Chesed, to ask for love and mercy and to pray for Grace, but there is a reluctance to face awe and fear of God.

The essence of Gevurah would thus appear to be destructive and fearful, but inwardly it emphasizes a fierce and tested love, such as that expressed in ascetic practices. Just as many things that give the appearance of Chesed turn out to be its opposite, so this feeling that Gevurah is inimical to our welfare is a delusion.

The direct Light (Chesed/Abraham), for all its abundance and infinite goodness, reaches some edge where there is no more reception. All descent has its limit. The ascending Light of Gevurah (Isaac), however, has no limit. Unlike the restricted capacity to rise on earth, for every mountain has its peak and every man his mortality, the ascent of Gevurah is indeed infinite.

One may ask: Is not God's mercy without end? The answer, of course, lies in the fact that the giving does not remain in the realm of the abstract. When Chesed becomes connected with the specific needs of those who receive grace, each according to his place in the value system of the World of Action, it can no longer bestow without measure. The abundance can become a curse, like flood when the blessed rain keeps on falling. This, in the Kabbalah, is the "breaking of the Vessels," what occurs when the Light exceeds the capacity to receive it. Does not everyone experience the smallness of the capacity to absorb pleasure? Do we not cry out, "Enough or I bust!" even though we feel that our desire is measureless and our need immense? For man is a fragile vessel.

Thus the very finitude of the vessel restricts the downpour of abundance, and divine Grace has to restrain itself (with the aid of Gevurah). If one teaches something that is too much for the pupil, one has really not given him

171

anything at all. This does not mean that it is impossible to give unstintingly, it means that the limitations of the receiver have to be considered. Chesed and Gevurah have to circumscribe each other, each helping the other to be what it is. Yet ultimately it is Gevurah that is infinite in its power. Chesed, the direct Light, diminishes and narrows in its descent whereas Gevurah, the returning Light, keeps getting broader and fuller as it ascends.

The boundary of Chesed is very definite, even if it is not always clear whether at the edge it can be called Gevurah (and vice versa). But of course it is not a matter of terminology. The point is that when Chesed gets to a certain edge, it ceases to be Chesed and becomes something else – like when a mother forces just another spoonful into the mouth of the child who has had enough. And when Gevurah does set a limit of some kind, as in the laws of the state, its severity may often be considered an act of kindness, even if not intended as such.

"Rachamim" (Pity, Compassion) is another name for the Sefirah of Tiferet (Splendor, Harmony) and corresponds to Jacob, the third patriarch. It is more than just a synthesis of Chesed and Gevurah; it is a definite Attribute of extremely subtle and varying qualities. In terms of our present thesis (on the ultimate meaning of Gevurah), suffice it to say that Rachamim combines the direct Light and the returning Light by putting the emphasis on the receiver. Indeed, it is probably even more orientated to the object (of goodness and love) than to the subject, for the object of compassion is what makes compassion meaningful. The whole value and purpose of pity lie in the wretchedness of the one who cries out for it, not in the "need" of the one who offers it. In fact, the greater the distress, the more compassion is evoked, and where there is no misery, one may not find much pity around.

With love, on the other hand, the principal factor is the lover and not the beloved. Of course, there has to be an object of love, but the relationship between subject and object, lover and beloved is much less dependent on circumstances. Indeed, there can be a feeling of love for practically anyone or anything. Compassion, however, is more narrowly defined and more restricted in scope. It is not directly connected to the vertical flow of above and below. In Kabbalistic terms, then, it corresponds to Jacob, the middle line, the line of harmony or the hinge upon which all else turns. It is not readily given to crisis, as are the Attributes of Chesed and Gevurah, which have their own enormous problems precisely because of their extremism – the tendency to go to the utmost in love or in fear. Rachamim thus seems to possess a scope that almost reaches from end to end, except that it depends so much on mutuality. Chesed is dependent entirely on the giver; the lover is the decisive factor. And Gevurah, too, does not pay much attention to the needs of the other; what is central to it is the rightness or ultimate perfection of a detail in the wholeness that is ever widening.

Which brings us back to the statement that "Isaac is our father." The returning Light rising toward the infinite is also a movement to its source, who is our father. Whether it ever reaches the goal is irrelevant; what is crucial for us is the aspiration, the reaching out toward the ultimate.

And now we approach the other part of the strangely weighted meaning of Isaac, for there is a double personality concealed in the enigma. Even his Hebrew name, Yitzchak, means "He who will laugh" and is derived from his mother's declaration, "For God hath made laughter for me, everyone who hears will laugh on account of me" (Genesis 21:6). What is meant by laughter here? Why is Isaac himself also laughter, in spite of the utmost seriousness of his outer personality and, as we have seen, in spite of his significance as returning Light?

To better understand the scriptural logic, let us turn to another instance, taken from the Talmud. In the Tractate Taanit there is a passage concerning Hanina ben Dosa, whose wife asked him to plead with Heaven to be given a little of the portion due him in the life to come. After getting what she wanted, she regretted that she was diminishing his portion in the future life and she asked him to pray to rescind the request and to have that which he had received to be returned. He did so, and what had been bestowed on them disappeared. It is then said that greater is the latter miracle than the first, because the Heavens only give and do not take. The great difference between the Kingdom of Heaven and the Kingdom of Earth is that from the Heavens there is only a giving.

According to the Kabbalah, the four Worlds emanate from Atzilut and become Briyah, Yetzirah, and Assiyah. The direction of their emanation is always from the less dense, from the nothing to the something, from that which has the capacity to emanate to that which is emanated – in other words, from essential emanations to creations, to formations, and finally to that which is "made" in the material world of Assiyah. The order of the natural flow is a descent, or a diminution of grade. It is a general process from a higher world to a lower world. From this universal rule one would see the order of creation as an influence from above to below – the Light always comes down, the source or halo is more than that which is illumined, the cause is greater than the effect. In short, it could be gathered that there is a fixed order in the physical as well as the spiritual worlds in terms of direction; the higher influences the lower and there is no opposite flow from the something to the nothing, from the below to the above. Anything else not only would be contrary to Divine order, it would be absurd. How could the Light return, and how could the lesser give back to that which emanated it?

We glimpse here the meaning of the Bible statement, "God has made laughter for me; every one that hears will laugh on account of me" (Genesis 21:6). The laughter comes because of the upsetting of the established order, the breaking of the rules. God Himself has turned the tables and the effect on one is that of absurdity and incredulity. Such reversal of the ordinary is the very essence of a good joke. So long as the Creation proceeds from above, it is characterized by a certain propriety and even solemnity. But when someone pushes in the opposite direction and there is an inexplicable thrust from below upward, it seems preposterous – not only laughable, but even improper and embarrassing. "God has made laughter for me."

A similar refrain may be observed in a passage of the Song of Songs (6:5), הסבי עיניך מנגדי שהם הרהיבני, "Turn away thy

175

eyes from me, for they have overcome me." The meaning of the Hebrew word הרהיבני here is more accurately that which "made me big" (instead of the usual translation of "overcome me"), as though to say that your eyes have expanded me, augmented me to the point where I am no longer myself. Since this is not proper, there is the request to turn away your eyes from me. According to the order of things, the influence should be in the opposite direction; there should be an augmenting from the lover to the one who receives love. But when the lover is himself enlarged by the beloved, the sequence is upset.

The true order is thus from the Divine giver to the creaturely receiver, and the recipient giving something back seems to be against the design of the universe, even though it may be a matter of great joy to overturn things in this way. Moreover its absurdity may contain the elements of an exceedingly great mystery and wonder. The unprecedented action against the current may be more than a matter for surprise and dismay. Like the effect on one of an inert object that lifts itself up, we are not quite sure whether to laugh or to protest. We do not even have an adequate way of describing the sublimely absurd. We are like the angels who complained to God about His preference for man: "What is man that Thou art mindful of him." And God agreed that man was indeed an inferior creature in comparison to the celestial beings, but there was something so ridiculously poignant about human efforts to "talk" to the Divine that God could not help but be touched.

Man can thus be viewed as God's plaything. The fact that he can turn to God is so amusing and even wonderful that

God keeps him close – is mindful of him. And because man is able to lift himself upward, against his own nature, in contrast to all the other creatures of the universe, he may be considered as participating in spiritual process. This is the aspect of Isaac, both as the returning Light and as the nullification of being, as the crystalization of form and as the ascent out of form into the infinite source of all being.

True there is the creative process that produces something out of nothing, which is generally known as "nature." The world goes from above to below, but there is something in man that makes him do otherwise. When Choni HaMaagel is asked to pray for rain and the rain comes in such torrents that he is asked to stop it, he is reluctant to do so, and he apologizes to God: "Your children are not able to receive neither so much of goodness nor so much of evil." But Rabban Gamaliel sent for him and rebuked him: "You are like a son who marries before his father does." In other words, how much can man presume? How much can man ask of God to take back what was given and how much can man himself return the Light from heaven?

All of this is not just an intellectual play around the name of Isaac – "he who will laugh" – and the doubleness of the severity of Gevurah. Basically there is no contradiction at all. In a certain sense, it is perhaps the purpose of it all. The laughter depicts essential joy, the highest pinnacle of this world where man shows himself as the unexpected response to Creation, the creature who strives to give something back to God. And God is amused: "He has made me laughter."

God's name in the left line of the Chart of the Tree of Life is Elohim. This aspect of the Divine points to the endeavor to turn darkness into light, tears into smiles; it is also that which combines with the name Havaya (I am that I am) to form the aspect of both Rachamim (Compassion) and Din (Justice). That is, all genuine release and pleasure are manifested through some combination with this aspect of Divine reality. As it is written: In the future, living waters will come forth from Jerusalem to the eastern sea. This eastern sea is the Dead Sea, whose waters are now so salty that nothing can live in it. In this image of the future, the order of nature will change, and the living waters, which are in Jerusalem, will flow to the eastern sea, the place that never has enough water. Jerusalem will irrigate the whole world with life, even the eastern sea of death.

From this it may be presumed, according to the esoteric revelation, that the world will go along a course opposite to the usual, and the living waters (which is also Isaac) will flow into the desert wilderness. Since in the present world God is always giving, and therefore "losing" something of Himself, there has to be constant replenishment from the original source. But as a rule there is no replenishment, so in fact there is less and less reflection. True, some of the receivers may be aware of what they get and even give thanks. Few realize that the point of severance, where reception comes to an end and another world of content begins, is precisely the point at which one may also requite God. It is the crucial place of passage and the point where the blossoming can start, but it also has a severe and threatening aspect.

Indeed the aspect of Gevurah that expresses control, contraction, and the urge to withdraw from the world does have its destructive side. Most men experience trepidation when confronted by the challenge of Gevurah. For men are able to give to the world the things it lacks, but it is difficult to know the greatness of receiving and control, of giving back unstintingly and thereby rising to a higher level of relationship. It is therefore only in the ultimate future that Isaac will be our father, rising higher than Abraham, when Gevurah will be more than Chesed. There will be a reversal of server and served, of giver and receiver. The Priests will serve the Levites, and man will give himself to the Nothing, to the infinite source.

V

ELIXIR OF LIFE AND DEATH

14

Elixir of Life

It has been mentioned that the creation of man took place in two stages. First, man was formed as perfect and self-sufficient, corresponding in essence to Higher Wisdom (Chochmah Ila'ah) and to the Written Torah. Second, there was a division followed by the creation of woman as a separate being, which is of the nature of Binah, the Sefirah of Understanding, and corresponds to the Oral Torah. The original source of all is Infinite Light, and the process of Creation is a continual manifestation by means of both Chochmah and Binah, Written Torah and Oral Torah, characterized by a breaking down into ever more specific detail.

The original Creation had to provide the basic design as well as the raw material. Substance had to be given form, and the individual forms could be separated and identified. Indeed, much of ancient and medieval philosophy was devoted to the problem of primordial substance and form. The Golem, in its amorphous and human aspect, represented the incomplete, the still inchoate state of matter before Creation. Divine "interference" was the act of giving form, completeness, to this primordial substance, as exemplified by Man or by the Written Torah.

This inchoate substance, the still formless primordial matter, cannot be grasped at all. Only when it is given form can it be apprehended. Before that it is still potential – the darkness from which all things emerge, the not yet existent. In terms of the esoteric wisdom, it is at this level of Briyah that Creation took place through Divine utterance. In the hierarchy of manifest worlds, Briyah precedes Yetzirah and Assiyah; substance has to come into existence as the stuff from which everything else manifests. "Adam DeBriyah," or primordial Adam, is still only potential man.

It is only at the stage of Yetzirah, after the initial stage of Briyah, that man was created. At this level of "Adam DeYetzirah," the world as we know it begins, and Wisdom manifests itself through the Written Torah.

To be sure, there is a long, complex list of correspondences to this genesis procedure. To illustrate, let us take a modern metaphor, the electric battery. Before it is connected to an active circuit, it is only a theoretically possible source. The energy is nonmanifest, although it does exist somehow. We apprehend it only upon connecting the wires. The potential becomes existential.

The question we are here trying to answer is: Where does intelligence come from? Suppose I have an idea. From where does it enter my mind? Often we can say that it comes from someone else. But what about the situation of contemplating the sky and suddenly having a thought pop into one's consciousness? And there are times when we feel certain that the intelligent illumination has emerged from a level of existence that is not mental. That is, the brain is not a warehouse of intellectual constructions from which all our thoughts arise. We have to assume the existence of something greater that we are unable to locate specifically and that serves as a source, or store, of that which takes shape as thought.

This source is so hidden that we do not have a clear conception about its very existence. And this in spite of the fact that it is apparently the root of all meaning, the essence of idea formations. In certain traditions it is called the original or impenetrable Wisdom that manifests (at a lower level) as concept, and then as speech. At first it is potential, then there is the flash of intelligence or sudden illumination, which is still only a transition to a clearly defined thought. In other words, we have a creative process: from a kernel of an idea which is nothing that can be apprehended to a definitely conceived idea that gives light.

To return to our starting point, let us recall the two marriage blessings: "Blessed is the Creator of Man" (יוצר באדם) and "Blessed is He Who created man in His image" (יצר את האדם בצלמו). The first is related to Adam and to the Written Torah, the second to Eve and to the Oral Torah. The second also contains the preposition את, whose letters also spell the feminine form of "thou" and are the first and last letters of the alphabet. So this additional preposition contains all of the letters of the alphabet, all of the revealed world, and thus serves as a symbol of the Lower Wisdom manifesting itself.

One of the reasons why Higher Wisdom, or Chochmah

Ila'ah, does not manifest is because it has, as yet, no letters or words. For the first flash of intellectual illumination is still without words. Only afterwards do the words come, at the level of Lower Wisdom (or Understanding) within the framework of a particular language.

To be sure, the basic ingredients need not be words as linguistic components; they can be no more than symbols, such as those used in mathematics or music, each with its own "language." The important thing is the idea—and in the beginning of a thought, it is still without specific language, without definite symbols, notes, numbers, words, or signifiers. It does not yet have a comprehensive structure. It is related to what we have described as the flash of Wisdom. Afterwards this flash is provided with its symbols and forms, its verbal and conceptual structure. That is, the idea assumes extension and depth, takes shape and suggests various implications. There are people who are capable of getting such illuminations but are unable to "interpret" them or give them communicable form. On the other hand, there are extraordinary people who can conceive an idea in more than one kind of symbolic ingredient or "letters" and can even choose their own formulation, in whatever comprehensive structure they feel at ease with, whether words, numbers, colors, tones, or whatever.

Rabbi Nachman of Breslav is said to have declared that if people were able really to hear his teaching, the melody as well as the words, the dance of it, they would be released from the bondage of reality. In other words, the same idea can be expressed in words, in music, in movement. There is a basic ground for correspondence of things, a fundamental unity behind the variety of modes of expression or symbols.

In any case, Chochmah, or Higher Wisdom, does not have letters, whereas Binah does possess the requisite letters for manifesting the infinite Light. It is the relation, in essence, of Adam and Eve, Written Torah and Oral Torah, the process of progressive revelation. Chochmah, or Higher Wisdom, is itself primordial, a potential manifestation of infinite light. Only as the elemental substance is moved to become revealed does it express itself as a flash of insight, a luminous idea that can thereafter be put into words.

It is written that God created man in His image, that is, man was given the form of a certain image. If the second manifestation of infinite Light is Lower Wisdom, which is expressed as the revealed world, this manifestation is the image of the image, the revelation of the revelation, the result of actualizing the potential. As the blessing puts it: He fashioned from Himself an everlasting dwelling place. In another context, it is written that the feet of the manifested world go down to death. This statement implies that there is a problem with this physical world if it tends to drop to the lowest level, even to death. But because there cannot be a place or level of existence that is entirely cut off from the Creator, what we have here is only a point of separation, when "its feet go down to death," when the material world gets to the other edge of existence, where it meets up with evil and death. The manifestation of Lower Wisdom still remains the emanation of Infinite Light from Higher Wisdom.

Because the original flash of Wisdom is a wholeness, too much is concentrated as in a point. What is expressed is still not humanly "understood." The world of Briyah is the stage where general Wisdom begins to be broken

189

down into details so that we can know what it is that is revealed.

In the subsequent breakdown, some parts are bigger, more important, or more independent, and each by itself can be used in a variety of ways. For example, let us take the "Shema Yisrael" prayer, which is a single idea of Divine Unity. If we break the declaration down into its separate parts, each word, like Shema (Hear) or Yisrael (Israel) or Echad (One), becomes a concept in itself with its own infinite associations, uses, and combinations. We can even break it down further, into its letters, which, as phonetic integers or symbols, have an even wider range of "independence" and usage.

In short, the world of separation, whose "feet go down to death" (Proverbs 5:5), is the inevitable result of breakdown of any wholeness into detail. The process of particularization can go in any direction but ultimately it tends to get out of hand; endless analysis, or breaking things down into their components, leads downward to eventual meaninglessness, or death.

Nevertheless, the world of separation, or a universe made up solely of shells, is not the aim of Creation. It is rather a by-product of the independent nature of reality, a result of the fact that each world has its own existence and that the Divine withdrawal that enables things to maintain an apparent independence tends to extend ever further into reality and allows for inevitable decline. And this in spite of the fact that the fundamental purpose of the breakdown into detail of the original unity was to make for a greater clarity, a greater understanding. Wisdom needed to build a more solid structure in order to stand up to the negative influences of reality.

To understand this more clearly, we must realize that Genesis is a single and pure act. It cannot be distorted, and it also cannot be transmitted. In order for man to receive it and manipulate the world, it has to be broken down into parts. This breaking down allows for distortion, an inevitable result of the freedom to make use of the parts.

Indeed, a structure is already a consequence of Divine concealment and withdrawal. For light to be revealed, it has to be clothed in substance and made specific in terms of an object to be apprehended. The original idea has the advantages of perfection and durability, but if it is to be transmitted and understood, it has to be "clothed," given words and letters, symbolic ingredients (language) appropriate to the intended receiver. A language is the mode of communication.

The original idea was not in any definite language, of course. Hunger, for example, is a primordial sensation; what one does or says to satisfy this need is of a secondary order. The language to express it has to be communicable, the actions taken have to be practical, and all of this is restrictive. Any original light loses its universality when it has to be transferred. The more it branches out into detail the more it loses of original unity and meaning.

The same is true for the reception of Higher Wisdom. It is written, of the Children of Israel at Sinai, that all the people saw the sounds. One may ask: How could it be that they saw the audible and heard the visible? We are accustomed to distinct systems of reaction to stimuli, each sense having its own nervous apparatus and brain connections. Is there not an organ of reception that does not bother about the receptor, a profoundly acute brain center where distinguishing and understanding take place? Could this not be stimulated directly? If so, it makes no difference what the channel of nerves or the nature of the reaction to a perception; sounds could be "seen" and sights could be "heard."

This is possible because the infinite Light is without limit or definition. It cannot be put in any particular category; it cannot be grasped except if it is contracted and "clothed" by something finite. As the Maharal says in his discussions on the Rambam: According to the (intellectual approach) of the Rambam one should perhaps speak of the Mind (HaSechel) as Blessed Be He instead of the Infinite (Ein Sof), which has no possible definition, certainly none in terms of human knowledge and wisdom.

As the infinite Light comes down and is revealed in one manifestation after another, there is also a descent in spiritual terms, a lessening or diminishing of essence. It is, as said, a process of breakdown into components, a division into detailed parts, an ever-increasing particularization which by its very nature leads to more rigid limitation and increasing distance from the general. To be sure, the purpose of the descent and the breakdown is precisely that–to illuminate those lower levels of existence, to bring light to the dark and "covered over" components of creation. In order for the illumination to take proper effect, the tremendous flash of light has to be broken down into details small enough to be received, specific enough to be understood.

It is written, God wishes to provide for Himself a dwelling place below. An ordinary person may wonder:

What for? To this a certain Tzadik once replied, "Concerning the secret desires of the heart, it is not advisable to probe too much." Nevertheless, the question lingers. Why should the Lord of the Universe want to live in the lower (in and close to man) worlds? Especially since doing so necessitates such enormous restriction, such a vast degree of contraction and specification. After all, men are really quite limited in their range of perception. Most vibrations, physical, electromagnetic, emotional, spiritual or whatever, have to be "translated" into simple communicable language. Higher manifestations are scarcely ever apprehended, much less understood.

To repeat, the aim of the breakdown is not to perpetuate separation, but rather to make a permanent structure that will perpetuate unity and make possible Divine manifestation. The means for this are paradoxically the outcome of concealment. In order for the Divine Light to manifest in the world, it has to pass through the vessels of hiddenness. That is, there has to be a substantial lowering of intensity, decrease in volume. Like for example, the need for transformer stations to reduce the current between the central power house and the consumer of electricity.

The reduction or contraction of Light, stage upon stage, is the means whereby manifestation can take place. Clearly this contraction also includes the process "whose feet go down to death." Alternately, the process is intended to achieve a structure, a kind of illumination or enlightenment.

This idea brings us back to the theme that Torah can be an elixir of death as well as an elixir of life. If a person does not obtain the privilege (or right) to study Torah, the study can do more harm than good. It does not depend on intellectual level, persistence, or anything else of an external nature; it is a matter of one's fitness in terms of receptivity. It depends on the heart's intention or sincerity, as expressed in the blessing prior to study. Thus, since it does not depend on the intellectual attainments, the elixir of life is available at any level of comprehension.

There are two ways of receiving Divine influence. One is in the objectively meaningful occurrence of a higher essence pouring down on one like rain, and getting "wet" irrespective of one's feelings about it. The rain, or the downpouring, also has no preference in the matter; all are equally granted the grace of what is bequeathed. Regardless of whether one is going to the synagogue or to the movies – the rain comes down on each and everyone. After all, the Higher Wisdom in its broadness and universality is equally available to all; each person can be conscious of its pouring down upon him and then cling as best he may to the spiritual influence. This clinging to holiness, or to Wisdom, is also a conscious adherence to (participation in) coming and going, thinking, speaking, being one with things. It is an objective holiness, an essence that accompanies one's actions, thought, speech.

In the second way of receiving Divine influence, the person enters another essence. On one side is Torah and Mitzvot and objective holiness; on the other side is the person, the subjectivity. If the person is not "privileged" to imbibe the elixir of life, if he has a wrong approach to the Divine influence in Torah, it becomes its opposite. It is not enough to sit and study, to lay Tefilin, to pray. There is also the subjective choice, the inner approach, leading to the elixir of life or death. The choice, though scarcely conscious, can make people exalted or secretly resentful. Because in addition to many obvious things, there are always other factors, buttons to press and valves to turn, which unless done correctly make it possible to receive something very different from what was expected.

To sum up, there's the objective, automatically benevolent downpouring of influence which comes down level after level, reaching a definite point, which is always the here and now. And there's another factor, of either being privileged or not being privileged to receive, of being offered a drink of life or one of death. That is, we are given a world of spirit that is pure and whole, and then we are presented with a level of existence whose "feet go down to death."

This level of existence, "whose feet go down to death," can be pure enough, but in spite of its having been derived from a highest source, in the end it does descend to death. Why? Because one who is involved in Oral Torah, which is Lower Wisdom, has descended to the "world of separation." That is, the active essence of the Oral Torah is opposed to the essence of the Written Torah, which cannot be spoiled or harmed or even changed. We can approach the Written Torah only on the level of the letters, its basic components, and we cannot get to the deeper meaning of the words. As soon as one enters into any sort of interpretation, one is in the field of Oral Torah. The difference between Written Torah and Oral Torah is not like the difference between Mishnah and Gemara and Commentary; any manner of giving Bible some understanding makes it automatically Oral Torah. The Torah is Torah Bektav, Written Torah; it is the basic Revelation, the ground for understanding, but it is not given to complete comprehension. Whatever understanding we have is Oral Torah, or interpretation. Oral Torah is a mixture of higher and lower, of God and man.

For instance, if someone who does not even know the meaning of the words recites Psalms, he is engaged in Written Torah. He is dealing only with the letters of the text (even though he may not even be able to read), just as the sofer or scribe, who copies the Torah letter by letter is involved with Written Torah. But as soon as someone begins to think about what the words mean, he becomes engaged in something else, in Oral Torah.

The problem seems to lie in the difference between contacting and connecting. In order for us to understand, we have to establish intellectual connection with Written Torah, and that is Oral Torah. The contact with the letters is not enough. The connection, which is Oral Torah, enables us to carry the Torah into our experiences of life. However, once involved with the world, one enters the realm of the princes of this world, the physical aspect of things, and this physical realm hides the holiness of the Infinite Light that comes from Higher Wisdom. Higher Wisdom clothes itself in Lower Wisdom, so that man is liable to be brought low and made to fall. Once the Torah gets into the world, one begins to see hidden meanings and not the real contents. One may lose interest and shake free from real content. Or one may even claim to relate only to the esoteric. In any case, one can do what one wishes with the Light, distort it, make it into that which is not Divine. At worst, it can be made into an elixir of death: if Torah is not an elixir of life and ceases to be neutral, it tends to become something else.

196

Whatever the relation becomes, it is as Oral Torah that it develops. Because interaction is the keynote of Oral Torah, things have meaning and power. As soon as one understands the words that are part of Torah—*sky, earth, sea, talit, tefilin, ox, donkey*—they become part of the world. With these components, one creates interaction. But if I fail to follow the right path, I may miss the contact with the Divine Light and come upon only the external components, that is, the ox and donkey. As such, they do not have much significance in terms of holiness. They cease even to be relevant and tend to nourish the shell and that which leads to the quick descent to death.

Here we come to the point where man is restored to the picture. After the giving of an objective Written Torah, after the great inspiration of the Divine Presence, there is a return to man, the one for whom all this was intended. Who is he, and how does he relate to it all? The way he relates is, after all, what determines whether the revelation is an elixir of life or of death.

In the final view, then, there is nothing that will function properly without discrimination. The figure of the man who takes it on himself to engage in Torah becomes crucial. True, there was perhaps a long period when this question was not pertinent; perhaps there was not great enough need or interest. However, the modern Chasidim did inquire. In what direction is one going? Man becomes the decisive ingredient in Torah. It is he who decides whether it is to be for life or for death. Just as any technological device can be ruined by a casual maltreatment, if a single error is made, intended good can become a great evil.

The Chasidim of ancient times used to prepare the soul

for hours on end before prayer, knowing that if the soul is not able to deal with the holiness of words in a certain context, the risk is very great. The man who dares to take this risk, who dares to defy the forces that lead to death, is the man who can make the Torah an elixir of life.

15

Elixir of Death

The Sages have been well aware of the many sides of Torah. Whether it is an elixir of life or an elixir of death depends on whether the person who occupies himself with it is pure in heart and is open to receive what it confers.

Why should the way a person relates to Torah be so decisive a factor? After all, the Word of God should be strong enough to overcome any obstacle. But we come to Torah through Oral Torah teaching, which is still in the limited context of the Lower Wisdom. This Lower Wisdom, by its nature, leads to the "World of separate things," where division rules.

This world of separation is said to be ruled by seventy princes, each with his own kingdom. That is, the world as we know it is a divided earth, with a multiplicity of forms of material existence and a variety of influences governing these forms. It is the princes of this world who determine the influences that guide all our actions.

When we are engaged in Torah, we are generally involved with the tangible aspects of its holiness. The inner essence of Torah is too much for us, so we suffice with that which concerns physical objects and comprehensible concepts. All that is deeper, more inward, or esoteric may be gradually penetrated by the initiated, but for the most part it remains unexplored. The Torah itself is a message to all men, however, and as such is concerned with this world. The objects about which the Torah speaks, especially the Oral Torah, are objects of everyday life. As for the Torah of the celestial spheres, as it is said, we do not have the contact with it.

This contact is out of the question because we are not a part of the higher worlds. We must remember that the Divine Light in things is beyond our powers of perception. Instead of seeing the Divine luminousness, we get consumed by the objects of the material world, the world of separation.

That is to say, while engaged in Torah, with its complex integration of inner and outer, holy and profane, one may find oneself in a dialectic quandary between the Divine Light obscurely felt in things and the practical Halachic action required of oneself. Thus one can easily get caught up in a play of ideas about the various aspects of it all.

Therefore it is said that for the one who is not pure in heart, who is drawn to that aspect of intellectual play in the world of separation, the Torah may be an elixir of death. If, instead of relating to the Divine Wisdom at the root of Torah, one seeks only the lower revelations, a division results between the manifest and the esoteric, between the inner essence and the outer expression of the text, and the

Torah one is occupied with is no longer the Torah itself. It becomes instead an extension of one's own little world.

When one is thereby thrown back into the world of separation, one is subject to the shell and the "sitra achra" (the other side). True, this too is a creation of God, and one may claim that God should be to some degree responsible for me even in that state. There is Divine responsibility for all created things, above and below – the birds and beasts and the angels. All beings have a well-defined place in the fixed hierarchy of the universe.

In such a hierarchical world there is always a crack or opening through which the holiness can be apprehended. Thus whichever creatures need such can get nourishment from that source. However, there can be weird misapplications of this freedom. An example was the mad Roman emperor Caligula, who appointed his horse senator. He may even have raised him to the level of consul – something which, even if in not so startling a manner, is not so unusual in the annals of government. It is all connected somehow with the subtlety of appropriateness in the realm of the holy.

If the holy is separated out or eliminated, the shells begin to get confused. The periphery of things becomes all important and the essence is lost. This is true, of course, whenever the external object becomes paramount and the inner content is obscured. Thus when the outer aspects of Torah are emphasized, the whole nether world, חיצונים or "externals," is allowed to penetrate life. And this is what we have termed the elixir of death. That is, the Torah is not a neutral realm of existence; if its holiness is not absorbed, it becomes a different influence altogether, poisonous and life negating.

As the evil impulse fastens itself onto what is studied, there is a severance of the Oral Torah from Higher Wisdom. The severance is an interior one, often not even recognized, but it manifests as an increased fascination with outer objects, with things, with technique.

Intimate contact is then established with the "klipah" or shell. And the shell begins to have its effect not only in the external sense, but also in the emotional life. Pride enters, and the domain of feelings becomes the center of one's being. It is most pathetic when such a person proclaims, "I have nothing but Torah," and in truth he does not even have that. The pious self-sufficiency of belonging to Torah is a sham if one does not live wholeheartedly with the holiness of Torah.

In other words, when a person makes something of himself and does not nullify himself before the Torah, his learning is of little consequence. If Torah study is not for the sake of heaven, it is no more than playing. Like those who claim that Torah sharpens the mind – might they not better play chess or use something else to whet the brain? That which does not repudiate itself before holiness cannot receive anything from it.

The effect of sanctity is to go out of oneself toward the other; I no longer want anything for myself. The self is relinquished and abandoned. The result is a spontaneous giving; the holy is always dealing out and bestowing gifts because it is not considering itself.

In contrast is an act of charity that is done, even if with the best of intentions, only because it makes one feel good. The shell is easily capable of identifying with an image of righteousness that enhances the self. To be sure, there are many degrees of such egotism, from the self-absorbed student to one who snatches what he can, or just opens his mouth to be fed while presenting a show of clean hands.

Holiness, on the other hand, is always giving. And just as egotism can be so intricate that it seems like something else, so too sanctity can be so delicate that it becomes another thing. For example, one can so ardently desire to be engaged in holy actions, that the satisfaction of experiencing it becomes more important than the action. One cannot help getting some benefit from all the holiness one is dispensing, but, as Rabbi Akiva is reported to have said, it is perhaps better to wait until the recipient of one's charity resents you and heaps curses on you before feeling your own worth in the matter.

The moral here is obviously not that there is a seemingly masochistic ingredient in the process of doing good. Rather it is that one should recognize the perils involved in sanctity. One may sincerely wish to do something very grand in the realm of the holy and at the same time to feel something of the grandeur of what one is doing. In this case, one is doing it for oneself, a sign that its origin is in the shell, for the klipah is always egocentric. The shell in fact can be defined as that which is constructed as a private world around the ego.

When a person is not nullified before Torah, the Torah becomes an independent force not bound to Halachah, and thus severed, it allows for all sorts of interpretations, even the most brilliant, all of which end up as aspects of the elixir of death. Even if the sanctity of Torah and its Divine revelation is recognized, so long as one is engaged with only the external facets of Torah, its visible and obviously ethical message, one is still missing the point. It is not the Divine Torah that thus engages one; it is something similar, that looks like it.

The important factor seems to be the quality of the intention of the heart. Only that which is awakened as an above from below is the higher spirit. It is not the subjective aspects of a person occupied with Torah, what is in his mind or in his emotions, that is important. Rather it is which Torah he is relating to, the Divine or the "human." What counts is accepting the holiness of Torah as obligatory Halachah because it is Divine Word. Even if one grants an objective sanctity to Torah, if one can still insist on one's own version, then the Torah ceases to be holy.

How does this elixir of death operate? It does not occur when someone makes an error in Torah; it happens when a person tries to fix it up or when he finds all sorts of wonderful things in it and makes them his own. Gradually the book becomes adjusted to him, becoming *his* Torah; eventually it becomes the Torah of the world, and then a vehicle of the shell.

How can we keep ourselves from such impurity in relating to scriptural source material? This is a very real problem, both for those who do not engage in Torah and mitzvot for the sake of heaven, and for those who are genuinely sincere in their relation to the Oral Torah.

It is the Oral Torah that is the key, because it is not something to be received in complete passivity. It demands responsiveness, in terms of intellectual understanding, doing things, asking practical questions, and building superstructures. The Oral Torah is not only to be studied; it demands the person's whole life and personality.

At the same time the question remains: How is the student to keep himself from sinking into the worldly aspects of the Torah to such a degree that the sanctity slips away? The problem is not one of choosing either to attend to the Divine Word or to accomplish fine deeds. The problem is in the fact that it is almost impossible to be in two levels of consciousness at the same time. The consciousness of the Oral Torah, in its wider scope, is basically intellectual and requires a specific kind of thinking. But it also has a devotional side. Keeping the right balance between them is difficult primarily because they cannot be experienced simultaneously and because experience is needed to keep from excess in either direction. Accomplishing this is probably much easier for the simple-minded person who just says his prayers with great inner feeling but does not try to penetrate the words. When one is seriously engaged in learning Gemara, on the other hand, or when one has to pronounce judgment in a litigation case, the intellectual demand is uppermost; one is required to concentrate on a specific sentence in the Talmud or the Shulchan Aruch, and not on the blissful joys of holiness.

The thing that can prevent a person from entering into this arid realm of reasoning to the point where holiness is forgotten is the seal of Divine Truth, the recognition that the Torah is God's Word; it has His signature. The shell of life cannot penetrate this seal. Most prayers are sealed in this way with the words, "Thou art blessed, O Lord. . . ." The occupation with Torah is to let Light enter into one's being and not to darken the soul. It should be an elixir of life. And the problem is the way one approaches the Torah – which means to use the blessing as a seal or a protection (against the shell).

There are a number of books being published with a certain prayer to be recited before study, in order to emphasize the holiness of the Torah. The great Sage the Maharal once asked: Why is the earth getting lost? Because the Torah was abandoned. What does it mean to abandon Torah? The answer is that the Torah is abandoned if one does not bless it before coming to it. God seems to overlook many sins and trespasses and even crimes, but He cannot forgive the failure to bless the Torah. This blessing takes the Torah out of the category of just learning.

When Torah study is just learning it tends eventually to become an elixir of death. Not reciting the prior blessing exposes the Torah to the shell. Indeed, all trespass is simply such a disregard of holiness, the disdain that leads to blasphemy. For example, the sin of "avodah zarah" (idolatry) comes from the error of giving the respect due to God to something or someone else. The essence of sin is sacrilege, the mistake of making that which is holy into that which is profane.

Let us say that there are many different worlds and there is a corridor running through them, like a thread, which is never spoiled. In all the worlds there are distortions, variations, but the one thing that remains fixed throughout is the Torah. This Torah somehow gets to our world, so that we are allowed a passage through to holiness, to the holy of holies of reality. When a person offends the Torah, it is a far more fundamental offense than anything else. If one is struck or injured, the pain is transmitted to the brain just as every sensation gets to the brain and to the heart, but there is a hurt that strikes the nerve directly and this is the most painful of all. In this way, to offend the Torah by failing to recite the blessing means to make the Torah a thing, diminishing its holiness. And the more one is engaged with Torah in this profane manner, the greater is the injury to holiness, until the Torah is no longer able to serve as a means of nourishment for the world.

This protective seal is first of all a protective device from above; everything holy has to be watched over. The Oral Torah requires a very special relation, one that even imperils the soul, for the Oral Torah leaves itself open to that which is impure. It has so many devious branchings and side passages that one has to make special efforts to get out. These extensions are of the very essence of Oral Torah because it is something given to man to use. The Written Torah is primarily of a higher essence. There is also a Torah that is human, something man can do with as he likes, for his own amusement, so to speak. There is human involvement with this Torah, but a problem arises when this involvement becomes a means serving *my* ends. At what stage does man become the essential factor? Is the direction of the flow inward or outward? When a person is in a state of holiness, the more he gets the smaller he feels himself to be. With one in uncleanness it is the very opposite; he more he gets, the bigger he feels himself to be.

In this respect, what is one to do? On one hand, as it is said, there's a seal above; on the other hand, there's a seal below. A person has to say a blessing for the Torah, as for all the aspects of holiness. He has to concentrate the direction of his thought from himself to Torah, the word of God. This seal of the blessing will allow the Torah to remain in its own holiness even though it is being given over to man, to human manipulation.

16

Overcoming the Obstacles to Lower Unity

Just as the effect of Torah study depends on the attitude of the person who is engaged in it, so does the work of the heart, such as Love and Fear of God, vary according to the individual's inner being. For we can distinguish two aspects of the heart, the interior and exterior. The interior is the passion and zeal of Divine love, its joys, and the overflowing goodness that comes from contemplation of the Infinite Light that is the source of all that exists. Among the manifestations of this interior aspect is a clinging of the soul to God as a vivid reality, not necessarily as an idea. It is the relation of the higher soul to its fundamental substance and source—a recognition of that from which it has come and which sustains it. As the soul contemplates the Divine in this way, its ardor increases.

Thus the soul can approach God and establish a relationship with a living God who is the Lord of the Universe, that is, one makes contact with a sensible Divine reality. This is made possible because of the factor of Wisdom or Chochmah. As it is written: Who is wise? The one who sees the birth of things, the one who is aware of the process whereby the world is formed.

To understand this, let us presume that we have two ways of seeing. One way is seeing that is not necessarily that of wisdom; it is a matter of simply seeing things as they are. Whereas the wise man can see the way things come to be what they are, their development and growth from something other. He can know the essence of things by observing their origin and growth. The first way sees the status quo, reality as it is presented to one. The other, that of Wisdom, is seeing beyond that which is manifest to the senses.

Having seen the birth of things in the world, the wise person is able to be free of the delusions of the world. Much of the strangeness and incomprehensiveness of the world comes from our ignorance of the process by which things happen. If a rabbit is pulled out of a hat, it is astonishing only to those who did not see how he was put in. Those who see the world only as it appears to them, as *the* truth and *the* reality of things, are confronted with a world that seems to be firm and unrelenting; to them, there is a world that is real and there is a God who is somewhere beyond it. The eyes of Wisdom, however, observing the process of events, are able to see reality in a more comprehensive way. They have become aware of another sort of reality, a world that is not divided and does not constitute a barrier to God.

The ability of the interior heart to penetrate to the essence of things thus belongs to Wisdom. Frequently, however, there is the sense of a great barrier, of distance and obstruction. But this is the product of an illusory belief in the reality of these obstacles. The more one believes in them, the greater they are. As soon as one is able to see beyond the immediate hindrance of the process, it ceases to constitute a barrier; one overcomes the illusory sense of vast distance or impenetrability between oneself and the truth of things. Upon which the soul can feel restored; the severance caused by the soul's descent to the body is bridged. Indeed, the barrier or distance is seen as a distortion of vision and not anything real, and the result is an integral awareness, seeing a wholeness instead of separate parts.

An old Jewish story may illustrate this. The inhabitants of Chelm are said to be a hopelessly dull-witted lot, and a Chazan (Cantor) is, more often than not, characterized as a swaggering fool, and among the domestic fowls the turkey is seen as strutting stupidity itself. We now have the turkey of the Chazan of Chelm before us and we want to cage him in so that he won't escape. All we have to do is draw a chalk circle around him. The turkey will be convinced that it is an impassable barrier, and he won't even try to get out. He will be imprisoned by his own folly. Were he ever to cast doubt on its imperviousness, there would be no problem about his freedom. It is a barrier only so long as he believes it to be real. For man, the chalk circle is our encirclement by all our worlds. This barrier consists of the sense of great distance between the soul and its Divine source.

It has been said: Day will speak to day like a gushing spring whose waters keep uniting with it. And so can the joy of the soul in God continue and run into Wisdom. That is, when the soul becomes conscious of the delusory quality of its obstacles, it will feel itself as a continuation and an expression of the fountain, its Divine source.

This reassurance that one has not ever been banished, that

one is actually in the same place, the very same place that one desires to be, is a great joy. Which happiness is the presence of God. In His nearness we go beyond the good or bad things in life, we are joyous in the Divine proximity. This is the ultimate happiness.

We are only too well aware of the opposite effect, however, the distortion, deception, and interference with the experience of Divine closeness. Such are, for example, the factors that divert attention from the integrity of study of Torah. There are also factors that may be called "unclean," that have no part at all in holiness. These forces are sometimes similar in appearance, so that one may err and go into a mansion that looks like the right one of the King and find oneself lost in a series of distortions. In just this way, many poisons act harmfully when they make the mistake of combining with molecules that give the impression of being right for them. Even in the physical realm, there can be erroneous identification of what is nourishing and what is injurious.

The joy of the higher soul, on the contrary, cannot err. The level of soul called "Yechidah" is not clothed in the physical at all; it is constantly full of the Light and joy of God. Whereas the animal soul partakes of all the worlds, especially of the body, and is thus exposed to uncleanness, the higher soul does not relate to the body, at least not in the same way, and its joys are of a different level.

Nevertheless, we have to admit that not many people are able to reach this level of unerring Divine bliss. Most men are prone to mixtures of physical and spiritual sensations and are unable to make precise distinctions. For instance, one feels the satisfying feeling of Sabbath holiness when, on Friday evening, one has washed and changed into holiday clothes and enjoyed a good meal and rested a bit. But an identical feeling could be experienced on Wednesday, if one washes and dresses up and eats well and rests. Could then the feeling of Sabbath holiness be a delusion, a sum of purely physical sensations? The trouble is that there is an inbuilt mixture here of the experiences of the body and the soul and it is not easy to separate them.

In the case of Shabbat, the mixture is not dangerous; it is even essential to the joy. In other cases, however, it can be dangerous. For example, in the event of great exultation, a person might feel he has suddenly reached a very high plane of spiritual potency. Indeed, any imbalance in the mixture of the worlds is apt to cause trouble. One may learn this lesson from the instance of Rabbi Elimelech, who ordered his Chasidim to refrain from wine and liquor during the latter part of Succot and especially on Simchat Torah – and this precisely because Simchat Torah is a special time for joy in the Torah. According to Rabbi Elimelech, if the joy of Simchat Torah is mixed with half a bottle of vodka, there may be some difficulty in distinguishing it, because the sensations are similar. As one of the Sages remarked, a person who takes pleasure in good food on a feast day is often enjoying his belly and not the holiness of the occasion.

Thus the feeling of joy in some outer spiritual circumstance will have its parallel in a physical source. Because the physical sensation can be the same for both, there is a lot of room for imagination and error. A person can imagine he is on some high plane of sanctity and actually just be puffed up with pride. The sensation of spiritual achievement may very well be no more than an enhanced appreciation of one's ego. To be sure, there are instances when the distinction is so grossly obvious that a person has to be cunningly able to deceive himself to get away with the fraud. But there are also cases when the differences are very subtle indeed, and there are no objective standards to measure oneself by. The purely subjective pleasure stands by itself in the midst of a question: Where am I? What is the source of my joy?

Again, let us take as an illustration the case of a man studying Torah. He becomes elated at having found something new and interesting, a "chidush" (innovation). And indeed the Torah may very well have revealed something marvelous to him and his joy may be a genuine intellectual elation unrelated to his ego. Or it may be a feeling of exultation at having gotten the better of someone else, of showing himself to be more clever, more successful than others. That is to say, it can be a joy of spiritual experience or it can be a joy of the shell. This person can continue to study Torah and keep enjoying the occupation with Holy Scripture while all the time be involved in idolatrous worship of himself. He can even be immersed in Torah in order to maintain a barrier between himself and people, because he dislikes people. Perhaps the more he shrinks from the people around him, the more intensely he will bury himself in study. Hatred of others can hardly be considered a basis for love of God and His Torah.

Oddly enough, this negative relation to the world can be expressed by a person going from one extreme to the other; an ardent political rebel such as a Communist can go to orthodox religiosity while remaining full of dislike for his fellow human beings. The question here is: Can there be any holiness in behavior that is characterized by hatred of one's fellow man, no matter how neatly it is covered up?

This problem, which touches upon the subtler aspects of the soul, is not as complex as it seems. The great joy that comes from the highest aspect of the soul, the Yechidah, is of a level that is beyond all else. It is a joy that is not like any other. It is essentially different from the common joys of men that are derived from one's relation to others: The great joy of the soul is a result of Divine union, a "devekut" or clinging to God; it is solitary, inner joy, a blissful selfness. It does not depend on outer circumstance, mood, or state of mind. This joy, known as "Ahavah Beta'anugim" (Love in Delights), is a state that needs nothing else to maintain itself, neither physical nor spiritual stimuli, being the joy of the soul in itself, in its clinging to the living God. And this state, this joy, cannot be contrived or counterfeited.

It has also therefore been known as the attribute of Day or of Light, as it is written: Day to Day utters speech, יום ליום יביע אמר (Psalms 19:3). To be sure, the Sages have explained that such a level of bliss is a gift vouchsafed to only few, such as Tzadikim and those of their calibre, that it is the soul's own light, and as such is even higher than what is known as a revelation of Elijah (גילוי אליהו). This "Yechidah" or "unity" of soul is perhaps the highest level of being attainable by man, outside of the domain of prophecy itself. The few who receive it feel the intimate nearness of the Divine, a sense that nothing can harm them. The truth that it expresses is timeless: Day shall express day, and it is entirely Light, beyond the problems of mind and man, outside the reach of sin. There is self-sufficiency in the presence of the Holy One, Blessed be He.

The interior aspect of the heart also correlates to light and to day, whereas the heart's exterior aspect may be seen as darkness and night. But the latter is not to be taken as a negation of the former; the Light is hidden, not absent. The exterior heart is the garment in which the higher soul is clothed in the body. One may say that it is the sensation of the soul's living in the body, with all the limitations and sensations and wondrousness of it. There is constant inter-action between soul and body, between spiritual elements and animal elements.

This interaction is possible because the attributes of the Divine soul, love and fear of God and so forth, have their corresponding attributes in the animal soul of man. We have a situation of rather precisely parallel worlds. And it is not a matter of the individual person of course; it is intrinsic to the very core of things, a part of the essential reality of the universe.

Thus, love, for instance, may be an expression of either Higher Unity or Lower Unity. The meaning of Higher Unity is that there is nothing besides Him. Lower Unity is a recognition of God within a framework of consciousness that assumes the existence of the world. They are two modes of grasping the Divine reality, but they are not necessarily contradictory. They are simply different experi-ences of God: The Unity of exclusive Divine Oneness and the unity resulting from a union with the Divine other.

Thus we are engaged in constant strife, in a state of struggle, because all that is above is to be found below;

whatever there is in holiness is also in the unholy. To get to the level of holiness, a certain struggle is necessary, a virtual war, like between nations in the womb of Rebecca when she was carrying the twins, Esau and Jacob. The twins are born with us, they accompany us throughout life, and they continue the struggle. As it has been written, were it not for God's help, we would probably not be able to overcome the foe. Every day the impulses of the lower nature come forth to draw man down to death, and he has to rely on Divine support to maintain himself. In this persistent war between fairly even sides, only man's constant choosing the good saves him.

Hence the great wonder of the soul's power to stir up love, to rouse it until the beloved becomes ready to divest herself of her garments. In truth, there is nothing totally separate within the realm of Lower Unity. God Himself always desires to participate when the soul turns to Him, when the love is aroused. There is in the love of the soul an urge to stand before the Divine alone and without any screens or veils. But even though one can desire this with all of one's being, the reality of the world continues to exist for one.

The world persists as an objective reality, as a crudely tangible fact that cannot be ignored. That is, there is a certain difference between not knowing that there are barriers and trying to overcome them by desperate effort. And this is the difference between Higher Unity and Lower Unity. In Higher Unity, there are no barriers; in Lower Unity the barriers have to be overcome.

It may be appropriate here to point to the Psalm of David that prays for a "uniting of my heart" (Psalms 86:11). Does this mean that there are two hearts, an exterior and an interior one? The two hearts, one of the aspect of day and one of the aspect of night, are certainly not separate, or divided, Heaven forbid. The difference is not a genuine difference of division, of two separate entities, each with its own borders. It may be likened rather to a situation in which something blocks one's view of the landscape, and on climbing a little higher, the obstacle no longer exists as a screen and everything is open to the gaze. True, that which blocked my view still exists, but from a higher vantage point it ceases to block. The lower view and the higher view are different; they are not the same, but they are certainly part of the one landscape.

Evidently, the aspect of night has something in it that manifests the aspect of day. That is, the exterior heart (the night) is the external manifestation of the interior heart (the day). The night is that which contains within itself the day; the night conceals and wraps up the day in itself, in order for it to become manifest and revealed. In other words, the hiddenness exists not for its own sake, but rather to be overcome so that the heart will be able to pass on to its other side. Its purpose is to reach that condition whereby the so-called physical heart, the human existence, is also able to hold within itself the essence from above.

This implies that the heart can feel within the confines of the body all the things that it can feel outside the body. This is so because the Higher Love of Delights comes down in stages to the human love in the heart which is expressed in the animal soul as well as the Divine soul. Man can thereby feel within the limits of the barriers all those things that he can feel outside the barriers.

If such, it seems, is the purpose of it all, there is no real division. True, there is a barrier of souls, but it can be overcome. In the upper world, one does not see the barriers, and in the lower world one has to learn not to pay attention to them. In the nether world, one finds oneself in another state, in which one has to learn afresh how to see things. As the Sages once put it: The soul learns the wisdom of the Torah in the womb before birth, and at the emergence into external life all is forgotten, so the soul has to spend the years of earthly existence in relearning it all. Thus proper study is also a process of recollection, not an absorption of new knowledge but a remembering of what was somehow once known. To be sure, every soul is faced with a unique context of life problems and although one reaches the same conclusions, the process is always new and fresh.

This brings us back to the two marriage blessings. Adam and Eve had profound attraction to each other as a result of the fact that they were once one. Two halves who seek to reunite is the essence of life and love, not the desire to know the other but to know one's self, to make for wholeness.

There is no easy way to reach Higher Unity, however. It has to be done by first achieving Lower Unity. One has to learn from the real life on earth, build oneself from the existing materials, proceeding toward the "other" and achieving wholeness.

Those who try, through tricks and stratagems, to avoid the arduous work toward Higher Unity often reach something very different—neither higher nor unity. Life in this world has to be gone through, and in such a way that the person is able to integrate his existence in the world with the Holy One, Blessed be He. A person who accomplishes this

223

can then try to make the transition to another level of reality.

In short, if one cannot believe in a God within this world, one cannot recognize either this world or a God beyond the world. If one cannot see God in the world and together with the world, one cannot perceive any (Divine) reality at all in respect to which the world does not exist.

In the realm of the Higher Love, or Unity, there is no room for the shell, which is such a very separate and different existential entity. Nevertheless, the love and fear of God that exists in the body of a man and is expressed in the relations and contacts of the body does provide the shell with something to hold on to. There in the physical being of man, the shell finds itself a foothold and lodges itself, drawing nourishment from the higher forces co-existing in the same person.

Therefore, one needs something to seal the blessing – that is, a certain influence to obstruct the shell and prevent its causing error. It is very easy to err. One is exposed both to the holiness within and to that which is not holy. The forces of the shell can enter unobtrusively even though the person may be convinced that he is firmly fixed in the love and fear of God. He may be unaware of what is happening to him, feeling it does not belong to him somehow. All the more reason to be very careful.

Similarly, we have the impulse that speaks to one of Torah for its own sake, without the forces of the shell, and we are confronted with Torah that demands interaction. Both impulses are genuine in their love of God, except that the latter involves the action of the body as well as the soul.

Indeed, sometimes one is not certain who calls, so a person can get enthusiastic and inspired about something that turns out to be quite removed from the holy.

There is a story about a hermit scholar who devoted himself entirely to Torah and prayer in a little room which he never left. Once he thought he detected the sounds of an audience, of people quietly gathered on the other side of the closed door to listen to his devotions. He tried to pay no attention to this rustling noise, but he did experience a heightened fervor at the thought that he could awaken others to devotion, and he prayed more vehemently than ever. Thus he continued for months and years, until he felt himself on such a high plane of spiritual achievement that he could now show himself. He opened the door and found that the rustling noises he had been hearing were made by a family of cats who had camped there. For years he had been praying for one litter of kittens after another.

The capacity for self-deception is enormous. And if it is in the realm of holiness – not just a matter of playing a role – there is real danger as well as absurdity and folly. Therefore the need for a seal, a mark of truth that clearly delineates, and also that maintains correct proportion, a sense of the fitness of things as well as a knowledge of extremes.

Even though it cannot be said that setting limits is the main purpose of the world, there is no denying its necessity for the sake of reality. In man there is a process of selection: he absorbs certain things and rejects others. So long as a person can discriminate, both physically and spiritually, all is well. But when a person comes under the corrupting influence of luxury, the situation changes. The need for limits becomes urgent, both those that come from above and those that come from below. From below one can be concerned with one's own private realm of action. But in addition, the power to awaken from below can stir the higher awakening, the higher consciousness of limits.

There are blessings that do not need a seal – those blessings that belong to the higher world, that deal with lofty matters where there is nothing that can be harmed. But when the blessing relates to specific matters of people and situations, there is a need to seal it and set up clear lines of demarcation, because one has to be careful not to burst the boundaries of things in the world and let in too much holiness.

The limit and the seal are somehow mutually dependent. On one hand, the awakening from below stirs a response in all the worlds, and on the other hand, a bursting of boundaries from above allows man to make his own limits, cut out his own territory.

There is a part of every blessing that also gives room for freedom of action, providing an opening for man to make his own space. True, the blessing also has a capacity to spread out, to get to the wrong place and be used as a source of pain and suffering. Its influence can be transmitted in the wrong direction – either by becoming mechanical or by a slight change of proportion – because we live in a kind of symbiosis with the shells. So long as things are kept within proper limits, they do not cause harm, but when these limits are broken and their influence extends into dangerous areas, the shells grow like a parasitic force, so that we have to fix rigid boundaries. It is like the walls built around a city to keep out the enemy. When there are no enemies, the walls are superfluous; rigid limits are needed only to defend and to define.

Thus a blessing has its symmetry of beginning and end, an opening and a seal that closes it. But the problem is not just external. Man's reality is such that the blessing may have its effectiveness dispersed in all manner of ways. The blessing needs its form and limits so that a person should be able to be free within its boundaries.

VI

FAITH AND PRAYER

17

On Faith and Blessing

The blessings we normally recite daily and on special occasions were for the most part formulated by the Knesset HaGedolah (the Great Assembly) in the time of the Second Temple. One may ask: What about the Jews of the period of the First Temple? Did they not have blessings to say in the normal course of things? The answer, it seems, is that their faith was so ingrained in their being that they did not need to recite blessings. Philosophers and research scholars may have trouble discerning this notion with their intellects. Historically, at least, Jews are a people of faith, children of generations of faith, and their grasp of certain basic matters is not easily comprehensible to the more rigidly rational approach.

Altogether, faith, in its essence, is beyond the mental grasp of the human mind, and perhaps even of the soul. It belongs to a realm of existence higher than our normal scope of cognition, where reasoning does not seem to be much use. Similarly, in the physical life we may know a sensation of nameless fear without any reason; we may experience the inexplicable or visionary. Yet faith is much higher even than these mystical experiences. And even if the intellect is needed to make God comprehensible, it is not the mind that grasps God.

It therefore cannot be a simple matter to explain what faith is. It may be appropriate first to relate to its contents. The faith of Israel is primarily a belief in the one God who is more sublime than anything that has form or that can be conceived. This faith rests also on providence, on personal Divine grace, on a particular relation to the individual person and situation. This is the problematic faith which the research scholars cannot quite grasp. Indeed philosophies of all sorts, including those that take pains to prove the existence of God, have trouble with this problem of the relation between the world and the Divine, between personal providence and Divine essence.

According to the Baal HaTanya, the people of Israel, devout believers and children of a long tradition of faith, receive and absorb this faith from their earliest years. It is not given to analysis or reason; it lies rooted in the depths of the soul. This fact implies that the commandment to have faith is rather absurd. How can such a "mitzvah" be ordered or commanded? If one has faith there is no need for the mitzvah or commandment to believe; if one does not have faith, the commandment can have no effect. It is not a matter of making an effort. In contrast, the mitzvah to love, for example, may be considered difficult for those who do not love naturally, but it is certainly not absurd to demand it. Perhaps the mitzvah to believe is a directive to recognize that such a mitzvah exists, but one either believes or doesn't believe, regardless of the mitzvah.

It may be argued, therefore, that this mitzvah is really a commandment or an injunction to know and not necessarily to believe, a matter of the intellect and not the heart. But a descendant of the Baal HaTanya, the Tzemach Tzedek, undertook to expand this idea and gave it his own formulation. He claimed that faith is the unification of the world with "Sovev Kol Almin" (a Kabbalistic concept of that which Encompasses All Worlds), that they are both the same. The mitzvah to have faith is a commandment to believe that the Lord (YHVA) is God (Elohim); it is not a commandment to believe in the existence of something one cannot perceive.

On the Day of Atonement, Yom Kippur, all the prayers come to their final consummation in this conviction that the Lord is God. This belief, uttered at the end of the day, the philosophers cannot grasp.

Indeed, we cannot grasp it either, even with all our powers of thought. We believe because it is a part of our essence, as the Baal HaTanya points out, because all of Israel are children of a heritage of faith. It is said that in the time of the First Temple, the souls of Israel were at such a high level of attunement with the Divine Light that this infinite Light, "Or Ein Sof," radiated in them and was apparent to all beholders. The Shechinah was revealed, as it was described, in the fullness of sanctity.

The Hebrew word for faith is "Emunah," which is of the same root as "Emet," or Truth. So faith and truth are really the same word, or at least derived from the same root. To believe is to recognize the truth of something, and to admit a truth is a matter of faith. What we consider truth is almost always a leap of faith at some point.

235

The problem lies in the fact that not every level of faith has the same degree of clarity we require for certainty of truth; there are differences in the way things are believed in. Some concepts are clear, others quite vague. For example, items directly perceivable by the senses provide us with a clear faith in their existence. I can be more committed about the reality of a table before me than that of Mount Everest. Not that I question that such a mountain exists; it is only a matter of the distinctness of my certainty about it. The unquestioning faith in objects one can see and touch is different from the obscurity of one's faith in more abstract or paradoxical objects.

For example, there is the children's paradox of trying to envision that people on the other side of the globe are not walking on their heads. It takes some time and effort to distinguish the transparent truth of antipodes; not everyone accomplishes it with the same ease, although there is no real doubt in anyone's mind about it. In other words, there is faith that is clear as day, readily seized and easily grasped, and there is the faith that is not clear in this way, that has to be learned or at least worked at with mind or heart or both. A person may be very intelligent and even learned and still be unable to grasp certain matters of faith in their simple clarity. This obstacle is not connected with issues of good and evil, but is a consequence of one's powers of abstraction, or rather of seeing certain kinds of truths clearly. What may be obvious to one person is often beyond another person's perception, just as one person has the ability to see a joke whereas there are others for whom no amount of explanations will help.

Of course, the capacity for faith is not in the same category as a sense of humor or a feeling for esthetic beauty. It may have something of the essential quality of inwardness, beyond the intellect, but it is far more profound, since it is not only a matter of the mind but also, to a powerful degree, a matter of the heart.

At the time of the First Temple the higher soul predominated in the quality of Israel's faith. This level of soul has a more intimate sense of the truth. It is characterized not by an intellectual grasp of the world but rather by a deeper and more immediate apprehension of the truth. There was also a greater degree of Divine revelation at this time, or at least it was more objectively apparent. Altogether, then, there was a clarity in the world, and particularly in relation to holiness. Faith was obvious, and Divine reality was a familiar and general experience.

Philosophers and research scholars have a problem not only with the idea of a spiritual relation to God but also with the relation to the self, the I. It comes down to a definition of the self, grasping its essence and all that this involves. There is probably no one who has any doubts about the reality of his own self, even though he never saw an "I" with his senses. The "I" is an immediate inner certainty.

We are saying that sometimes the grasp of the Divine is similar to such an immediate certainty. And in the time of the Second Temple, when this certainty was the norm, the sages of the Knesset HaGedolah fixed these blessings as an ongoing expression of faith. The blessing evinced the reality of their spontaneous mode of belief.

To be more specific, the opening words of the blessing,

"Blessed Art Thou, O Lord," is an extension of the Infinite Light of the Divine downward into revelation. There is no definite form, only a steady downpouring, an action of the same root as "brechah" (pool), to gather together and draw to a point. The meaning of the word blessing (Berachah) is to draw, to pull down, continue, or project Divine influence to oneself or wherever.

Every blessing has its own particular focus. There is a blessing for bread and a different blessing for vegetables; they are not interchangeable. There are also blessings for various mitzvot. All blessings have a certain structure consisting of a fixed core, which addresses the Divine Presence, and then a diverse content defining the object to be blessed. They all declare the same thing in many ways. I express gratitude and bless my existence, my condition of the moment, my food, or my performance of a mitzvah, and I adjust the contents of the blessing to suit the circumstance. The core, "Blessed Art Thou, O Lord," is the essence of the blessing, its underlying message. The point of a blessing seems, therefore, to be the declaration of a certain relation to God. All the rest is detail relating to a specific situation.

The blessings are thus an extension of faith. Their formulation seeks to direct the path of Divine projection from above to a congruent reality. The opening words, "Blessed Art Thou O Lord, our God, King of the Universe," define a vertical line descending from the "Thou" who has no name, who is beyond all titles, to the Lord God who is King of the Universe and integrally immanent in the perceptible world around us. After this opening come the various particulars. The blessing thus contains within itself all the elements of relationship with the Divine, expressing the inscrutable difference and closeness between the infinite reality, the transcendent "Thou," and the immanent King of the Universe. This relationship between the Divine "Thou" and the King of the Universe is the essence of the tension (and power) that we put into the blessing.

Another element in the structure of the blessing is the strange shifting from second to third person, from the direct address to God as Thou, to a statement about God as He. Sometimes, as in most blessings, this shift takes place in the same sentence. "Blessed Art Thou, our God, who sanctified us with His commandments." This is part of the Divine projection or flow (up and back) from the revealed to the hidden. It may be seen as two crossing diagonals. "Our God, King of the Universe" (second person) is directed to "He who brings forth bread from the earth" (third person). It is a double movement of the close and the distant, the revealed and the hidden, that which is before me and that which is beyond in the Divine "He." As one Sage put it, it is only one aspect of the difference between a "this" and a "he."

Every blessing thus has its structure and order, proceeding from a revelation of Infinite Light that the Lord is our God with whom we have a concrete, emotionally filled relationship, to the specific contents of the blessing which are personal.

How is this possible? It is because the souls of Israel are of the inwardness of the worlds, in contrast to the angels, who are of the outwardness of the worlds. The plane of the outwardness of the worlds, to which angels belong, is said to be separated into four rivers, or four archangels – Gabriel, Michael, Raphael, and Uriel. The one great river going forth from Eden ends up in four worlds, and this separation is the division between the inner worlds and the outer worlds, between the mixed world and the distant world.

The Sages maintain that there is a difference in the amount of time it takes for different angels to cover the world. Michael can cover it in one flight, Gabriel in two, Elijah needs four (because he was once a physical creature), the Angel of Death uses eight – each has its own "velocity" so to speak. But there is no rate for the souls of Israel, because a living soul is not so encumbered by the earth. It is of another dimension. The angels are still bound to the world, so it takes time for them to move in it, whereas souls are on a plane beyond earthly measure and so the world cannot limit them. The soul does not need any time to cover the world because the world does not exist for it. The relation of the angel to the external worlds is not at all like that of the human body, but it is still a relationship. On the other hand, the souls which belong to the inner worlds do not have any relation with the external worlds and are not effected by their form or size or the like. It makes no difference to the soul, for the soul is of another essence; it belongs to the infinite, the timeless, the unlimited. The angels – lofty as they are in many ways – have no such boundless essence.

What is being demonstrated here is that the people of Israel are of a tradition of faith, the essence of whose spirit is Divine, and therefore they can achieve more than other creature of God, above or below. They are capable of recognizing things that others cannot see.

The blessing addresses the Lord God as the King of the Universe, referring to the fact that the world is a manifestation of His Kingship. For there is no King without a kingdom. In this sense, the world is the manner in which Divine Kingship, God's sovereignty, is put into practice. When God decides to be King there is created a world for Him to rule over. The kingdom emanates from the King and expresses the King. It has no other essence. Its existence depends on its relationship to God. The situation may be likened to the logic of numbers: 1 does not need another to be itself, but 2 needs the 1 in order to be second. The very essence of 2 requires a relationship based on 1. And this in turn is the inner contents of "Lord God, King of the Universe."

The meaning of all blessing, then, is to express and make the faith manifest. Every blessing is a plea for God to reveal something of His own Self.

On the whole, blessings are worded in the plural: *our* God, who commanded *us*. That is, they are expressions not of the individual but of the collective, and they are directed toward a general situation. We might mention here that before his recognition as a great teacher, the Baal Shem Tov used to engage people in the most casual conversation, asking them, "How are you?" "How goes it?" and the like. When he was asked why he did so, he replied that he only wanted people to say, in formal response: "Baruch HaShem" (Blessed is the Lord). Every Jew who said this phrase, honoring the Holy One Blessed Be He, raised the throne of the Almighty, making it firmer and steadier. But in addition to the general contents of blessings, there is at the same time the individual who turns to God and who receives something in return; at least a portion of the blessedness comes back in the performance of the mitzvah. There is a drawing down of sacred current.

Just as the mitzvot are instruments to induct the Infinite Light, so too do they serve as means for this Light of the Ein Sof to descend and extend holiness into the world. And this is the reason for the next words of the blessing: "(Lord) who sanctified us with His commandments," אשר קדשנו במצוותיו. The word "asher" (that), translated here as "who," points to a relationship, and it is open to a variety of meanings. Basically, it is a causal factor, the one because of whom something took place, or who provided it with significance. That is, the opening statement of the blessing—"Blessed art Thou, Lord our God, King of the universe, who sanctified us with His commandments"—is not a declaration that something exists, it is rather an explanation of our relationship to Him *because* "He sanctified us with His commandments."

The blessing then continues with the verb formation "and commanded us," ציוונו, which has the Hebrew root צוותא (together), thus indicating a linguistic bond between the three words, commandment, or "tzav," צו, mitzvah, מצוה, and togetherness, or "tzavta," צוותא. The point of the action is not obedience as such but joining together, a unity with the One who gives the commandment. There are several levels of being involved. On one level, every mitzvah is a combining of three factors: man, who performs the mitzvah; world, or the action of the mitzvah; and God, who receives the mitzvah. Only when all three factors are in conjunction can the mitzvah be truly performed. The mitzvah is thus a bonding together of God and man.

Presumably, such relations can be produced in a variety of ways, such as in conversing. But in order to hold a conversation, there has to be a minimal verbal understanding, a mutual base for intellectual contact. Insofar as God is concerned, our limitations are only too evident; we cannot hope to understand His speech directly. He speaks to us, of course, and His speech is the creative power of our lives, but it is beyond our intellectual comprehension. We can grasp only certain limited forms of His address to us, the form of a clear-cut command to do something.

The relationship can be compared to communication with anything of a lower order: even though we cannot engage in a conversation with dog, we can make intimate contact by throwing a stick and calling him to retrieve it. Indeed, it is the togetherness of tzavta (צוותא) that is at the root of the mitzvah which is a response to Divine bidding. Therefore, in our need for communion, we recite a blessing to this effect, to draw the Divine Light down from above.

Another aspect of blessing is its concreteness. We express gratitude for the pleasure derived from a specific object or circumstance. I eat His bread, drink His water, enjoy all that comes into my area of experience. And the blessing creates a certain togetherness, a personal bond with the Divine Source. In a way, it is very intimate, more meaningful than words, because one understands the slice of bread in a way that one does not understand passages of Torah. God's speech is beyond me, but His address to me in this slice of bread is something I can grasp. We can see therefore that the blessing is built around a specific object and involves enjoyment of the senses in order to establish genuine contact.

Thus, too, the tendency is to anchor the marriage bless-

243

ings in something definite. As in so much of Halachah, the inclination is to extricate the precept from the abstract and bring it down to the objectively concrete. Most of the abstract blessings, like those establishing the holiness of a special day or the sanctity of marriage, are accompanied by a blessing on the bread and wine. The connection with the bread or wine creates a togetherness that is somehow substantial.

But the ultimate significance of these blessings is that they are a way of drawing down Divine influence. Every blessing first assumes that the power of God prevails over all and then proceeds with its own plea for Divine intervention, that God should "manifest" or somehow take part in this particular circumstance.

18

The Protective
Power of Prayer

The Talmud mentions that there are two different kinds of benedictions: the shorter type, which begin with the word "Baruch," Blessed (art Thou), but do not end with Baruch; and the longer type, which begin with the word Baruch and end with it as well. We may permit a surmise that they correspond to two different modes of reality – that of the hidden world, עלמא דאתכסיא, and that of the manifest world, עלמא דאתגליא. It is said that the manifest world originated when the four rivers in Genesis separated and became the worlds of Briyah, Yetzirah, and Assiyah. The hidden world is the one that is beyond cognition. This is not to say that in the manifest worlds which include that of Briyah and Yetzirah, the realms of celestial beings, one may meet and converse with bands of angels. The division into manifest and hidden is rather a division between what is above the World of Emanation and what is below.

These worlds below Emanation may be distinguished as Worlds of Separation, where separate entities begin to exist, as opposed to the unity dominating the world of the God-head. In lower and lower levels, where different forms are assumed, what is manifest is separate from the origin and connected to the shell of the Sitra Achra. However, it is still nourished by the origin, that is, the fragments still need to be sustained by the holy, so there is a continued dependence.

The Sitra Achra gets its sustenance not directly from the holy, but rather from the leftovers, the waste produced by the action of the holy in the world. These scraps, being a result of Divine bounty, of His abundant giving of Himself, are also precious. As was said of the pieces chipped by Moses off the Tablets of the Ten Commandments, they were each jewels of great price.

In another context, it is written, concerning the reward of Torah, "Length of days on the right, and wealth and honor on the left" (Proverbs 3:16). From this we may conclude that the Torah has two sides, right and left, and on the left the aspiration for wealth and honor seems to be fairly common. A Chasidic story tells of a certain pious Chasid who came to visit an old friend who had become a rich burgher. The wealthy host showed the Chasid around, greatly pleased with his house and his possessions. The Chasid finally told him: "You remind me of a certain animal that enjoys lying in the refuse and eating the leftovers from the master's table." That is, the waste is not of the essence of the holy, but it can nourish even at several removes of descent.

The manifest world which emanates from the Divine is so removed from its origin that it is full of fragmentation. Nevertheless, it still contains something clear and definite, a foundation that can be traced to its origin. For instance, the child in the womb develops all its parts out of a potential in the seed, growing out of the hidden, embryonic state into birth, which is a breaking out into the manifest. In the last stage of this growth is the development of the surplus, the hair and nails. The excess or waste growth comes at the end of the growth into wholeness.

In other words, the surplus was not there at the beginning; it accumulated in the process of giving life. When it all reaches the stage of manifestation, of fulfillment, the surplus will have come to its own separateness and wholeness. All of which hints at the (Kabbalistic) systems of joining, selecting, and winnowing out, the processes whereby that which is not absolutely necessary to the growth of life itself arrives at its own completion and is cast off. This process creates waste products. References to the days of the Messiah point to the time of purity; this does not necessarily mean that waste will vanish, but, on the contrary, all the various forms and creatures will have reached a certain level of completeness, casting off the surplus, and the burnt out ash. This is also true of certain chemical processes: when a new compound is formed, undesirable substances in the original composition are left as deposits. In certain psychological developments, too, the selection of true factors casts up a fair amount of error and illusion. Similarly in art or literature, the process reaches its finality with the rejection of the no longer necessary components. In short, as the distinction between outer and inner becomes clear, all the waste products can be disposed of. And this process provides the Sitra Achra with the leavings, the tangible alluvium of the holy, giving it sustenance and nourishment.

249

As for the Hidden World (עולם דאתכסיא), everything is contained in it, not only as a general unity but also as being on a higher plane of essence, and in an openness that may be described as sublime and perfect. It has no faults or deficiencies. Therefore there is no foothold for the hostile powers of Satan to fasten on to. At the highest levels of being, there are no openings for the demonic forces to enter.

The manifest world not only reveals something of the hidden world, but also brings to fruition the potential in it. Therefore, whatever was only a possibility of negative force or problematic life becomes waste. And the more pronounced this waste, the more it tends to serve as sustenance for all the forces of evil that, in their origin, belong to the world of intrinsic value.

We can now come back to the distinction between the shorter benediction and the longer one. The shorter one asserts only the essence of all blessing and very little else. There is only a request for Divine manifestation in a specific circumstance. Little or nothing is left for the Sitra Achra to get hold of; there is no excess to nourish the shell of being. The longer benediction enters into details, repeats the central idea, and renders a more comprehensive account of the circumstance. Room is therefore left for the Sitra Achra to maneuver; the hostile forces have more to grab onto. Therefore the longer benediction needs a seal, a definite closing that helps to keep it unassailable to these forces.

An analogy is the maintenance of health against the danger of disease-carrying bacteria. Most bacteria, of course, are quite harmless, having no relation to us, feeding on refuse and helping to disintegrate whatever has to be restored to life in different form. Some of them are even eaten by us, such as those in cheese. But we have to be on guard against contamination when the bacteria begin to attack the basic elements of our life, threatening the roots of our biological existence.

In any of our relations with the living world around us, whether with domestic animals or with men, we have to be careful to sustain the proper distance, knowing when to be intimate and when to separate ourselves. All closer involvement becomes an approach to the prohibited, like, for instance, eating the flesh of the donkey we drive to market. As for the inner world of man, in his feelings and thoughts the dangers of infringement are subtler and more dangerous. A little falsehood, for the sake of politeness and good neighborly relations, is often necessary, but if it is extended and corrupted by politics, if it insidiously enters the personal life and cannot get out, then it endangers the heart of existence. In other words, when the Sitra Achra is no longer satisfied with the normal waste products of life but begins to feed on the vital inner elements of our being, we have to make some serious changes. True, the point at which one goes from the harmless to the harmful is not always obvious. How does one know when the accepted fabrications of diplomats, publicity agents, or lawyers become dangerous lies? Or even the terse reports of military officers on readiness for battle or on victory? When is partial truth useful and when does it become a threat to life?

The problem lies in the slow incursion inward of what should remain outward as surplus and eventual waste. The sealing of the longer benediction blocks this process. Once there has been an opening for holiness to enter, it has to be protected, because it leaves room for many other influences to come seeking parasitic nourishment.

The very idea of a secret lies in its partial informativeness: enough is told to provide the chosen listener with the proper knowledge, but when the knowledge is made open to all, it becomes dangerous. Only a little detail may be sufficient for the few; too much of it can be food for wild conjecture and error. The seal is that which closes a truth so that it does not get out and become dissipated. It is also the signature of the me who writes, to keep out the intruder and dissuade anyone for whom the message was not intended.

Another metaphor, also inadequate, is various means of sterilization to keep harmful influence from penetrating into the sensitive core of life. The specific measures taken vary in accordance with the potential perils: whereas the hospital operating room must be kept strictly sterile, the neighborhood barber shop can suffice with much less sterility.

Much depends on what is considered vital to life. If the Sages felt that the dangers of drawing Divine power from above in an ordinary blessing were very great, they made sure to introduce a safeguard, such as Baruch in the final phrase. Of course, the safeguard does not function automatically; it requires the constant attention of the one who prays to continue the flow from the opening, to persist in his attachment to this source so that no room is made available to the forces of the shell. As it is written: "The Lord will watch over you," which indicates that it is a matter of encompassing Light, of God's protective enfoldment from above.

In a similar vein, there is a final prayer on the day of Atonement, Yom Kippur, which acts as a sealing device for the day, protecting the people from the inimical forces unleashed by the grandeur of the purification process. This process is actually a rising up to a very high level, reaching a confrontation with Divine reality. Before God shall you be cleansed. The closing prayer is also a seal for all of Israel and serves to secure the blessings of the people.

An anecdote is in order here to add substance to the meaning of such blessings. It is written that the first day of Succot (Feast of Tabernacles) is sometimes called the first day of forgiveness. Why is this so? Rabbi Yitzhak of Wurka, a Chasidic rabbi of some standing, is said to have given the following answer from his own experience: "I used to be a treasurer for a large estate and once, as I was closing the books for the year, it appeared that it had been a relatively bad year. I simply delayed the final statement for a couple of weeks, knowing that a particularly profitable deal was going to change the final reckoning. So, too, if we were to make our accounts with the Lord in the month of Elul, we would most likely be at a disadvantage. If, however, we postpone closing the ledger for a few weeks until after Rosh Hashanah and Yom Kippur, when we repent and atone for our sins, and then wait a couple of days for the first day of Succot, during which time we have little occasion for anything but the performance of mitzvot, then we have that much more chance of showing a profitable year. We can then begin a new account for the next year."

19

Prayer as Sacrifice

The Talmud has an interesting comment concerning the passage in the Song of Songs "Go forth, O ye daughters of Zion, and behold King Solomon with the crown wherewith his mother crowned him in the day of his espousals and in the day of the gladness of his heart" (Song of Songs 3:11). It is written in the Tractate Taanit that the day of his espousals is the giving of the Torah and the day of his heart's gladness is the building of the Holy Temple. This implies that King Solomon (Shlomo) here refers to Peace (Shalom), and the King of peace, who is the Lord, celebrates a wedding and a great gladness of the heart on these occasions of Israel's initiation.

But what is the meaning of these days of his wedding and the building of the Temple? The answer suggested by the Sages is that the gladness of the heart is the key, and the reason for the gladness is that "Prayer is instead of the sacrifices." This is not necessarily the same idea that is superficially taught in the schools, that after the destruction of the Temple and the cessation of the ritual, the prayers in the synagogue substituted for the regular sacrifices. This is not true historically or factually, not in relation to the First Temple, or even in regard to the Second Temple, for which we have much more literary and archeological evidence. That is, we have clear-cut remains of synagogues from the period when the Temple was standing, as well as the literary references to prayer as a customary practice.

Nevertheless there is a sound foundation to this idea of prayer as a development of sacrifice. The essence of both follows a similar vein. To be sure, there are those who see prayer as only a psychological gesture, the speech of a person turning to God and unburdening his soul. It is less costly than psychotherapy and enables one to express feelings and thoughts quite freely.

Prayer gives expression to two things. First is a certain gratitude, a thankfulness for something that is not necessarily connected to any particular event or circumstance. An Israeli archeologist once told me that he had found some words cut into the stone wall of an ancient cave dwelling: "I thank the living God. . . ." This was a spontaneous personal expression, like graffiti, without any connection to ritual or anything of a communal nature.

The other thing that prayer gives expression to is what is known as work, work in the heart. This work, also called worship, is *itself* ritual, and not *instead of* ritual. The Rambam asserted that prayer emerges from the Divine commandment, "And thou shalt serve (work for) the Lord thy God with all thy heart." In this worship as ritual, prayer is recited with the same intention as when the ceremonial sacrifices were done in the Holy Temple. In the course of time, prayer

258

as worship assumed psychological aspects, such as praise or supplication, which tend to become its finest expressions. Nevertheless, work is still central, and this concept was later defined to the extent that the world stands on three things: Torah, Avodah (work), and kindness. The word "work" as used here is very different, of course, from the term used by labor movements; its meaning is taken from the work of worship in the Temple, work that was considered basic to the continued existence of human society in a ritualistic sense.

Thus there is a ritual that is a physical act, like offering up a sacrifice, and there is a ritual that is work done in the heart. The fundamental meaning of all ritual, however, is sacramental, that is, it is not connected with anything that one personally wants to say. It has a formal structure, although one may add supplements for personal needs. A person prays, not because he has anything particular to say to God at that moment but because he has to do God's work in the world, and prayer as worship is an integral part of the ritual.

Prayer is thus the inner ceremony parallel to the outer ceremony of sacrifice. Rather than in the Temple, the ritual is performed today in the heart. Both ceremonies have been said to be שמחת לבו, "his heart's rejoicing." The synagogue is even today called a "bit of the Temple" of the Lord, scene of the rejoicing or gladness of the heart.

These three pillars of the world, Torah, Avodah (work), and Gemilut Chasadim (kindness), can be viewed as three lines of communication between man and God. The action of Torah is always reflexive, a continual entering into and going out, a constancy of mutual relationship. Prayer as

Avodah is a ritual action from below; Gemilut Chasadim is is an attempt to introduce holiness into the substance of the world.

Like the Torah action, the work of the heart has a circuitous quality. Since the heart is so central an organ in the body, the dependence on the heart is constant and vital. And the heart has two chambers, one receiving the blood from the various organs, and the other sending the blood back. The heart, therefore, can be considered the center of life, into which and out of which life flows.

Also the new blood produced from the food and drink that is consumed goes to the heart and thence to all the organs of the body. As it is written: "All the rivers run into the sea yet the sea is not full" (Ecclesiastes 1:7). Thus there is a parallel between the heart and the sea, which receives the waters and then sends them back. Indeed, the whole earth breathes and beats like a heart.

The spiritual work of the heart is also that of a crossroads, a center of all lines of force, through which life must constantly flow. Its cessation too is death. And its culmination is the Divine union, when the prayer mounts to such a level that the person who prays experiences the bliss of "devekut," the clinging to God.

All of this is possible because of the Divine spark in us. In normal conditions, everyone is occupied with his own affairs and this spark goes unnoticed. Prayer, however, offers an opportunity to let this Divine spark rise up to God, to make contact with higher essences. Although prayer is composed of many elements, and there are any number of ways to pray, the Divine spark is always present. It keeps returning to the confrontation with God, again and again.

Once more, to resort to a pitifully inadequate example, let us imagine that one is on a journey to a distant place but somehow arrives at another place. Then, picking up a telephone, one talks. What is said may be anything from the formally essential to the most trivial, or perhaps just silence. The basic reason for the telephone call was not in the message but in the establishment of communication. Similarly, the ultimate purpose of prayer is to raise that Divine spark which enables real communication to take place. It is an awakening of the spiritual in us and letting it carry us to the utmost of our capacities to cling to God in "devekut." This task cannot be done only through mental effort; there has to be an experience in the heart. This awakening of the innermost heart substance is the most important aspect of prayer.

To illustrate, one may refer to the principal prayer utterance: "Hear O Israel, the Lord is our God, the Lord is One." The opening call for Israel to hear seems to be no more than a rallying cry. Actually, though, it is a focusing of all the aspects of Israel, all the Divine Sefirot. It is a message unto itself, just as the following phrase, "The Lord is our God," is another whole message and "The Lord is One" constitutes a third. Each is a profound concentration of meaning. So the Shema (Hear, O Israel) is fixing a relation, a putting into contact of Israel (the human element) with Knesset Yisrael (the Divine manifestation). The mere fact of listening, of being in a position to hear, establishes the contact necessary for communication.

Such an awakening of the spark in the heart usually requires some preparation. It is difficult to make such a leap all at once, without any stimulation. Hence the "Pesukei

261

Dezimrah" (פסוקי דזמרה), a series of Psalms preceding the Shema declaration. Hence the need for a certain meditation and spiritual containment, with or without the Pesukei Dezimrah, to prepare the heart for its awakening in the Shema. True, a genuine stirring of the spirit may take place spontaneously, but this occurrence is rare, and often this too comes only as a result of some deeply moving experience, whether tragic or otherwise critical. In any case, a person is hardly ever aware of the influence of whatever stimulated the heart's awakening to God. It is like what is commonly called "love at first sight"; what seems so spontaneous is actually made possible by a lifetime of feeling and the soul's readiness. And so the focusing on "Hear O Israel" needs all the inner meditation and preparation that one can give it.

The inner meaning of the words, "The Lord is our God" is a union of Chochmah and Binah and contains a whole world of thought. It indicates this point of union between the transcendent and the immanent – the word "Lord" standing for the sacred name, the Tetragrammaton, which is also Havaya, and which corresponds to the reality beyond the substantial world, and the word "God" (Elohim) defining that which is in this world and makes up all its substantiality.

A passage in the *Zohar* says that with one thought were all the worlds created, and it is a matter of looking out and seeing to the end of all time in one survey. That is, the worlds are not confined only to space; all the generations of time are included. All of reality in all the worlds comes from one original thought, the point concentrating past, present, and future. Thereafter there is the breakdown into detail, into the specific things which make up the worlds in all their levels. This idea can be likened to scanning a three-dimensional object overall from a distance and then, only as one enters into it can one recognize details and measure the length, breadth, and height. At first there is the one all-inclusive survey of the whole. Afterward details become apparent; in fact, the closer one gets to the lower levels, the more particulars become available. And if we could conceive the notion of regarding a four-dimensional world, with time as the additional dimension, then we could have some idea of what is meant by the single thought that created the universe.

We now go back to the union of Chochmah and Binah, the essence of thought, thought here being the creative power of the universe. This union sees the world from the viewpoint of an inclusive survey of the whole, not as specific details or separate parts. The world is a compound essence, perfect and entire, and I am in it at a definite point. All the essences and aspects of this world join together at this point where I am, the point of union. It is the same as the flow of the blood to the heart, by which process all the organs come together at this one crucial point.

This primal union is that conjunction whereby all things come together at the first point without obliterating themselves, as the blood circulates back to the heart. All the specific aspects of reality are restored to this original thought. Reality ceases to be a mixture of thousands of details and reaches its point of unity. This oneness is what the Sages call the first movement, the beginning of the fundamental refrain or music. The emergence from the world of separation, where each thing exists by itself, to the world of oneness is but a single thought. It corresponds to the union of Chochmah and Binah, whereby the transition is made from the world of left and right, of space and separate objects, to the world of a single point, of one all-inclusive vision. Such is the initial movement of meditation.

We may define meditation here as the way one can prepare the soul for the experience of "devekut" (Divine Union). It is not itself devekut; meditation is only the instrument for reaching the aspired for experience of union. As the Ari is supposed to have taught, the intention every person should have in mind when reciting the Shema prayer is to offer up his soul to God as a sacrament.

The real purpose of devekut is to be restored to our Creator, to return to the source. A person offering himself up to God is surrendering his individuality, all the particularity of his own self. At the same time, he is in intention, in line, oriented to the one point of the Shema "call," which is the primal source.

20

With All Thy Might

In the primal thought of Creation, Israel rose to mind. The thought of the world and the development of the world in time include a great multitude of factors, of structures and systems. Most of them are secondary factors, structures that serve to uphold central realities that are the focal points in the whole. Israel is such a focal point, an aim and purpose of Creation. Or rather Israel is an expression or symbol of a certain perfection as designated by revelation.

Of course, Israel, the embodied people, has its own problems. As a detail in the whole, it wants to eat, to sleep, to enjoy itself and not be bothered with God. The purpose of existence, however, is to achieve a degree of perfection. Such has become the meaning and the function of Israel. Hence we say that the "Lord is God," Havaya, the primal source, is God in the world.

But reality includes the element of time and soul as well as world. The primal thought, as a point, concentrates all of time as well as space, and its development is called soul, that singular quality that gives everything its uniqueness and

267

meaning. The details are expressed in individual beings, even though in essence all the souls are one soul.

According to the ancient wisdom, there are actually five dimensions. Besides the three dimensions of space – breadth, height, and depth – there is the fourth dimension, which even in modern physics involves the element of time. The fifth consists of the dimension of soul. Any view of Reality has to include all of them.

If the primal thought of reality is a point, there is necessarily that which is beyond space and time. This is known as "Sovev Kol Almin" (Encompassing All Worlds). The encompassing is beyond the very essence of the worlds; it belongs to the Creator. Even though the human mind cannot possibly conceive of this beyond, we are required to meditate on it, trying to understand as much as the mind can grasp. To be sure, this may be said to be true of anything man endeavors to comprehend: true understanding is a gradual process of learning. Schoolchildren are not required to understand all the information they absorb and repeat. Meditation, as it is used here, refers to a certain mulling over and contemplation, a process of thinking about and absorption until understanding comes.

This does not mean that as a result of meditation, the subject is fully grasped. It simply expands the field of cognition, so that everything thought about, including one's ability to understand, becomes clear. The object under scrutiny passes the stage of words to the stage of contemplation. It has been said that no two people ever contemplate the same thing from the same plane of inquiry. Yet each person can, with his own faculties and within his own limitations, reach a certain clarity of understanding.

For instance, a child being taught mathematics can grasp addition and subtraction clearly enough so that he can be quite adept at it. A theoretical mathematician will study the inner laws and processes of numbers and eventually attain a higher degree of comprehension. Obviously, the understanding of each is of a different order, but the clarity is the same. It is the lucidity of perception that makes it possible to work creatively with the knowledge attained.

Similarly, a meditation on the words, "The Lord (Havaya) is our God (Eloheinu)" is intended to bring one to the utmost of one's capacity to understand. In practice it illuminates thought, adds a certain clarity to prayer. What is more, it leads directly to the following phase, "And thou shalt love the Lord thy God (with all thy heart, thy soul, and thy might)." Sincere meditation on the essence of God brings one to love. And we are somehow taken back to the metaphor of the beating heart, to the flow of blood constantly returning to the single point. The meditation on the Shema prayer is also such a returning, from the reality of the broad world to the focal point of Divine Love, from separation to unity. It is a movement of thought and feeling away from the outer and peripheral to the central and unified source of everything.

Thus, prayer as the work or worship of the heart has its two movements, its flow up and back. These are not monotonous and mechanical, however. Each movement in prayer is a song in itself, with rises and falls and secondary action, even as it maintains its direction to or from the center. The movement from the periphery to the center in the Shema declaration reaches to the words "the Lord is our God." The preceding movement consists of the Pesukei

Dezimrah, whose function is to prepare the heart for its takeoff. For one cannot expect a person to wake up in the morning, yawn, and be ready for this unique confrontation. Even for those who are fully awake at once, the heart does require some preparation. And each Psalm in the Pesukei Dezimrah has a function of its own, to prod and push the whole structure a little further in its spiritual uplifting. Each one belongs to another part of the soul composition and acts accordingly. Highly developed students of wisdom are conscious of this process and can order their physical and emotional responses accordingly, including the obscure nerves, muscles, and thoughts. An ordinary person reacts without conscious participation, but the influence of each section of prayer on a particular part of the being is a fact for all.

Altogether the recital of these Psalms is wondrously related to the various aspects of life and nature, but in their totality they are a song of praise to God. The function of the Pesukei Dezimrah is thus to reach a point where reality becomes an instrument through which everything empties itself into God.

We now come to the core of prayer, the "Shemoneh Esrei," the eighteen benedictions. It is the standing confrontation, the point of rising as high as one can go. Whereas the preceding prayers are just praise and do not ask for anything, the Shemoneh Esrei is full of supplication. It is an endeavor to draw down from above, a reaching out for things desirable below, whether it be knowledge, healing, forgiveness, or whatever. Mainly it can be considered a movement from below aspiring to draw upon the Divine Source and bring it down to the reality of this world.

In a way, the whole of "Torah and Mitzvot" as the way of life consists of this same endeavor—to bring Light into reality. There is no breaking up or rejection of reality; on the contrary, it is an adding to reality, an enhancement of that which is given.

This may appear to contradict the notion of sacrifice as a consummation, burning up of a part of oneself (unblemished object) in order to offer it up to God. But sacrifice is essentially an uplifting, a going up by offering or raising. Work or worship too is sacrifice, whether by prayer or mitzvah, and thereby a consecration of things, providing them with a certain holiness. Reality is not destroyed, it is enhanced; one fills it with light. If the first movement is that of offering up, of consuming the sacrifice, the second movement is the opposite, to illumine and consecrate.

This corresponds to the two movements of the beating of the heart, regulating the flow of the blood up and back from the heart to the various organs of the body. The mitzvot are known as the 248 organs of the King, and each mitzvah relates to a specific organ. Therefore a mitzvah without a corresponding "intention" in the body is without soul. Which is the reason for the statement that the blood is the soul. And every organ has its life blood or soul, which has to flow "upward," returning to source, as prayer.

Every mitzvah has its specific detail, as does every prayer. What is the function of the benediction in the mitzvah? A mitzvah, after all, is an action, even if an act of consecration, but it needs to be provided with a direction and this is the task of the benediction, no matter how small. This too is the "intention" (esoteric meaning) of the spreading and going forth of the blood to all the 248 (רמ״ח) organs. Malchut

271

(Sefirah of the Kingdom) rises and it also returns; it comes back to reality, which in this respect is the Shechinah, and it is like the blood of the heart that keeps running down to the furthermost organ in the feet.

The holiness, then, can come down to the very edge of death and darkness, to the lowest of the low. And even though man is sometimes in this extreme category of the lowest, the worst criminal or heretic does receive his life force from God, because the Malchut (Kingdom) descends to this world in order to correct it. It is not a descent in order to remain below. It is rather a process of introducing Divine influence into the world, a stirring of reality toward the Light. And when even a little spark is lit, is awakened to light, there is the beginning of a rising movement to the source of Light.

As it is said: From the middle of the darkness, at midnight, the Light begins to ascend. According to the hidden wisdom, the time of night until midnight is the period of decline, when the darkness gathers and deepens as the Malchut descends. But from that point of midnight, the time of the Tikun Chatzot ritual, the Shechinah is present and Malchut begins to rise. As the blood returns to the heart and the light is restored to the earth, there is also a union of male and female forces, of Chochmah and Binah, Aba (Father) and Ima (Mother), the powers of life and feeling. It is true for the Shema prayer.

The essence of what is here intimated lies in the concept of Israel as the heart of spiritual reality, capable of giving expression to the world's oscillation. In the great cycle of the world's pulse, its flow of spiritual life, Israel's task is to act as a vital center, as a heart of humanity.

If the circulation of the blood in the body is in order, the person may be considered healthy. If, however, there is some obstruction to the flow, either by a damaged organ or blocking of an artery, there is a serious crisis. Similarly, in the normal course of life when routine worship, or work of the heart, is steady and the prayers rise as they should, the soul may be considered healthy. To be sure, prayer has its own dangers of excess, when it rises too precipitously toward "devekut," when the soul aspires too intensely to Divine Union. Rebbi Elimelech was known to take out his pocket watch in the middle of prayer in order to resume contact with time and reality, lest his soul escape. But this is not a danger for most mortals.

The point is that prayer should be an offering up of oneself. The rest of the course of life, with its fulfillment of Divine commandments and common duties, has the opposite orientation of bringing down the holy into the reality of the world. Even if we do all our actions for the sake of heaven, as is enjoined upon us, even then the direction is from above to below, to bring heaven into the domain of substance. A person can do this with greater or lesser degree of completeness, but his task remains the same: to correct the world. This correction, adjusting or fixing the world, can be done in a variety of ways: by plowing the fields, repairing appliances, or exerting a more indirect or abstract influence on the world. Essentially it's a matter of adding some "light" to the density.

If this is done properly, the circulation of the blood from the heart to the organs, from Divine Union to the world, proceeds in some kind of harmony and rhythm. But if there is an obstruction to the flow, if in the course of living some sinful action or transgression blocks the channel, then sickness results. Sickness of body or sickness of soul lays a person low. And often, too, a whole variety of ailments strike at the same time, and a man is in great distress.

In the normal passage of time, the circulation of life and the blood can usually cure most ailments, even when there is much to be desired in the way of wholeness. The more severe blows of sickness and guilt are not so spontaneously cured, however. In these cases, special treatment is required; healing of the soul is a matter of repentance.

As the Sages have declared: Great is the repentance that brings healing to the world. And for all too obvious reasons, there seems to be a need for the special effort of repentance to help people overcome the many faults and weaknesses and obstructions in their lives. Even in the standard Shemoneh Esrei prayer, the eighteen benedictions repeated thrice daily, we say: "Forgive us our trespasses." And everyone says it, because there is no one who does not have his own defects and weaknesses. There are the saintly persons whose trespasses consist of not being aware of the Divine Presence all the time without exception. A story is told by the Seer of Lublin, one of the early Tzadikim, about his teacher, the great Rabbi Shmelke of Nicklesburg. At the beginning of their relationship, the Rabbi apologized to his pupil saying: "I may get immersed in Halachah teaching and rational explanations of the law, all of which is rather intellectual, so if you ever feel that I have forgotten even for a moment my devekut, clinging to the Holy One, Blessed be He, pull my sleeve." The Seer of Lublin concluded the story with the statement: "I studied with him for seven years. During this time, there was only one time that I felt I should pull his sleeve, but just as I was about to do so, he turned to me and said, 'Thank you, I have myself remembered.' "

So we have individuals whose transgressions and need for forgiveness are of this nature, and there are also those who have different problems, not only of the ordinary human failings. Many are spiritually ill, many in critical need of repentance. And varied as this factor is for different people, there is an aspect of repentance that is fairly universal, even if not always properly understood.

It is written: "And thou shalt love the Lord thy God with all thy heart (the work in the heart), with all thy soul (all the force of the vital being), and with all thy might." What is the meaning of the latter? With all thy might is that which corrects the deficiencies of the first two ways of loving.

To be more specific, "with all thy might" is a matter of giving something extra. For the most part, life is built on social frameworks, personal paths, and habit patterns. "With all thy might" refers to a bursting out of these defined limitations and doing something one thinks that one is unable to do. It is the person's breaking out of the confines of his selfhood and making contact with the limitless Ein Sof (the reality beyond space and time).

The essence of repentance is not restricted to a mere asking for forgiveness. "Sorry, I behaved badly." Repentance is a bursting out of one's ordinariness into an action that is "unthinkable" for one. A penitent, whether a Chasid or a scoundrel, is one who goes beyond the limit and does something he feels he could never do. This point is the

275

critical point of repentance. Repentance is the sudden impact of release when longstanding restrictions are shattered.

Repentance, then, is not mere regret followed by a (sincere-at-the-moment) resolution to be better. At the same time, repentance is available to all men, at any level of existence. As with any genuine healing, however, it means getting involved with the whole system, by taking a medicine. And all medicines have their "contraindications," their possible dangerous effects. Notwithstanding, the system needs a special counterforce to its unusual functioning, a medicine that causes some upheaval. Repentance is such a medicine. To be sure, it cannot be a permanent feature; it is by definition an emergency measure.

One uses repentance to get beyond the ordinary limits of one's world and reach a point that is Ein Sof, infinity. Everything is somehow pushed back into place. As it is said, repentance is that which precedes the world by becoming a part of the original emanation of Light from above. It shatters the confines of one's conventional being, so that "with all thy might" one can draw upon Divine power and accomplish what ordinarily cannot be done. As a result of this extraordinary effort, the one who repents can correct not only himself but also that which was faulty in the natural course of this life.

21

Beauty and Knowledge

Our attention is drawn to the passage in the Song of Songs (1:8), "If you yourself do not know, O fairest of women, go, follow the tracks of the sheep and mind your kids by the shepherds' huts." In trying to answer the intriguing question of what is meant by the beauty of women, we are led to the verse, "Rachel was beautiful and well favored" (Genesis 29:17), which adds to the wondrous many-sidedness of the question.

What is the precise definition of the words in Genesis: Yefat To'ar, יפת תאר (graceful) and Yefat Mar'eh, יפת מראה (well favored)? According to certain Sages, Yefat To'ar is beauty of form and limb, harmony of proportions and structure, while Yefat Mar'eh is more connected with face and color, with the delicate beauty of detail. To be sure, the difference has been elaborated and projected into many other aspects of both spiritual and intellectual beauty. So various people have been labeled as having a grace of soul, Yefat To'ar, or a beauty of soul, Yefat Mar'eh, and sometimes both.

Having ventured to mention the spiritual aspect of the beauty of women, let us make another leap and consider the long-held tradition that Rachel is Knesset Yisrael. Rachel, the graceful and the beautiful one, is not only a symbol of the Knesset (assembly or collective body) of Israel, she is, in a more profound sense, the very essence of Knesset Yisrael. And Knesset Yisrael, according to the Kabbalah wisdom literature, is Malchut (Sefirah of Kingdom), and Malchut is the Shechinah (Divine Presence on earth). On the other hand, Leah, the tender-eyed unlovely sister of Rachel, is the Divine matron, the Sefirah of Binah, which is on a higher level than "Rachel" in the Tree of Life.

The midnight prayers of Tikun Chatzot, which express the yearning of the people for God, are divided into two parts: Tikun Rachel and Tikun Leah. Whereas Tikun Leah is of a sublime character, Tikun Rachel is a weeping penance. Rachel is Knesset Yisrael below, the fallen or exiled beloved. She represents the reality of our existence and, in a very clearly developed tradition, has become the mother figure, evoking the deep appeal of this aspect of womanhood. Indeed, Rachel's tomb in Bethlehem has become a special place of pilgrimage and prayer for Jewish women.

One can speak in such terms because of the Biblical verse, "Let us make man in our image and likeness" (Genesis 1:26). Even the concept of the Divine Throne and the glory of the One who occupies the throne is an extension of this thought, as are all the descriptions of God's greatness, strength, splendor, power, glory, and so on. The Divine qualities are then projected onto the human soul, which is in His likeness. We are built according to a design that is of God.

But we are, of course, only a copy – and not a very good one. After all, how can one compare the limited human with the Infinite? True, man's soul does reflect the love that is Divine, but we are still finite. And the difference is not one of quantity; it is essentially a difference in quality, in the very nature of our being. The so-called likeness is not at all directly discernible.

Indeed, in order for man to be a repository for Divine Light, he has to completely nullify what he is. So long as he persists in being himself, he cannot be a Divine instrument or likeness, because he is of a different essence. By nullifying himself he can shatter the limitations of his being and let the Divine Light pour into his soul. To reach the love of God man has to get rid of love of himself; so long as he clings to his three-penny possessions there is no room for anything else.

Consequently, too, the prophet is not a man like other men – not because he is a mad or extraordinary person, but because he has thrown off his selfhood and become an empty vessel. He has become a vessel that God can fill and use. Moses was the greatest of prophets, able to speak with God because he was the humblest of men on earth. Because he had become nothing in his conscious existence, his existence could serve the Shechinah properly.

Nevertheless, there has to be some means of focusing the Infinite Light in the individual consciousness, and this is the "R'uta Deliba" (רעותא דלבא), the most inward heart's desire. It is not of the same dimension as the love and fear of God, which are in many ways an external relation to the Divine; it is more intimate and more rooted in the profound depths of being. One can be so impressed by the greatness and glory

281

of the works of God that overwhelming love is aroused, a love that is based on the admiration, and wonder, and gratitude for the supreme Creator, which love and fear of God has the quality of awe and worshipful respect. There is another kind of love, however, which is more like that between men in certain respects. Here the feeling leaps out of the fleshly covering and seeks expression in the soul. It is not given to definition; it is not based on admiration or awe. It is a relation to the very essence of the loved one. As it is written in the *Zohar:* "Thought cannot grasp Thee at all. But the heart's desire can grasp Thee."

An expression of this love is a certain radiance that is beautiful in a different way. Luminousness of soul can burst forth in an unexpected fashion: in a smile or a look that delights one, in a gesture that makes one forget that the person is really quite plain, even old or ugly. Where does this radiance come from? We may also be allowed to wonder at the nature of what we ordinarily call beauty of person.

In short, we return to the true heart's desire. What is it that is more precious than anything else to a person? Money? Pleasure? Power? As the Talmud story of Rabbi Abahu describes: His face shone with great beauty and joy because he had come upon a new explanation to an old Mishnaic text. The soul's fulfillment causes a radiance to shine forth from a person.

The priestly blessing says: "May the Lord let His countenance shine upon thee" (Numbers 6:25). What does this mean? After all, God looks upon all men on earth, and His Presence is always with us. But He does not always smile — and the invocation to let His face shine upon us is the expression for such a need. When we meet someone we love in the street, there is no need for words; immediately there is the smile of the heart's recognition; the eyes speak before the tongue has found words. The inner light is readily emitted. In fact, any opening for the fulfillment of the heart's desire radiates beauty.

In order for Knesset Yisrael (the abstract principle as well as its physical projection in a people) to be Rachel, the graceful and the beautiful, a certain process of passive acceptance has to be experienced. Israel has to become an instrument for Divine inspiration by an act of nullification.

But doing this, it seems, is still not enough. There remains the crucial question, "What is the soul's innermost desire?" To love, with all of one's life and heart, plus the extra bit beyond even one's conscious wholeness of being, may be as much as can be required of any man. Yet there is something else; that love, the heart's desire, be able to penetrate all the levels of existence, from top to bottom. The (poetic) image of God holding the world in His arms requires that He hold the lower depths in one arm while the other arm supports the rest of the world. Therefore any total change in the world requires a penetration into the fundamental basis of things, where the density is greatest and access is most difficult.

We are now led back to the phrase, "The fairest of women" (Song of Songs 1:18), which is supposed to represent the utmost of both "Yafeh To'ar" (beauty) and "Yafeh Mar'eh" (grace). This perfection is called the (proper) picture or the harmony of all the composite attributes, to the degree that the inner radiance emerges as irresistible beauty.

What is meant, however, by the preceding words: "If you yourself do not know, (O fairest of women)"? In other words, there is something that interferes with her complete knowing who she is; there are stages of this knowing, apparently, and some of them are at least in part unconscious. In this case there is room for not being sure.

The reply to this question requires a deeper point of departure. The Sages have taught that there are souls that are the seeds of Adam, who is the very root of human perfection. Coming from the soul of Atzilut (the Higher World of Emanation), they are born whole and they "know." Everyone with such a soul is fully conscious. An example was Rabbi Shimon Bar Yochai. Such persons are of necessity very rare. Even in the world below they are luminous with knowledge; in every experience, they are fully aware of all the aspects of the moment – where one is, what one is doing, and the consequences of doing.

There are other souls that are of the seeds of the animal and are not capable of the aspect of Knowledge. In order not to offend anyone, it may be appropriate to mention that this is true of all the souls derived from the other worlds below Atzilut, the worlds of Briyah, Yetzirah, and Assiyah. Moreover, not having Knowledge does not imply a lack of intelligence or sensitivity. The term is merely a way of distinguishing between greater knowing and smaller knowing; greater knowledge is one of wholeness, an all-embracing consciousness. Most men are of a level that is bound to earthly reality; they are structured by their sensual perceptions. And for the most part they are restricted to sight; the other senses are largely supportive. In any case, the chief factor of the seed of the animal is the biological basis. Man as man consists of certain levels of consciousness, and this includes an inner sense of things. The inner human sense (of the animal seed) may be said to be somewhere between the sense of taste and the sense of smell. His knowledge is for the most part thus restricted and so is his apprehension of reality.

The seed of Adam, however, has far higher potential, and meditation for such persons is a way to Knowledge; there is no need to perceive with the senses in order to "know." Most men, however, are of the level of the animal seed and correspondingly limited. Their intellectual capacities may be high, of course, but their knowledge is not derived from the spiritual dimension. It may be said of them, "If you yourself do not know, O fairest of women." Even if the soul is beautiful, the fairest of women, it may be incomplete, not sure of its knowledge, and therefore lacking something. This lack is of the nature of self-containment; one can know from outside and one can know with a knowledge that contains the known object, possesses it and makes it a part of oneself. Without this inner knowledge, one has to go out "and follow the tracks of the sheep." One cannot remain within the limitations of oneself if one sincerely wants to "see," to really know (God). It is necessary to go forth "and mind your kids by the shepherds' huts."

VII

SHEMA YISRAEL

22

Release from the Bondage of Reality

A Chasidic treatise on the day called Second Passover teaches us that nothing is ever lost. Even if one did not perform the Passover Ritual Feast as prescribed, or if there was some spiritual deficiency in the doing, or whatever – there is always the chance for Tikun, fixing and making restitution. One may spoil something, seemingly beyond repair – perhaps commit awful deeds or say unforgivable things – but nothing is ever really a lost cause. As has been described in Scripture, the children of Israel entered the Wilderness and stood before Mount Sinai on the first of the month, the time of the new moon, when the moon's light is so faint as to be almost nonexistent. The symbolism is clear. This is the mere initiation of a process, the preparation for receiving the Torah, corresponding to the three days of inner restraint and renewal imposed on the people (at Mt. Sinai) in order to receive the Keter or Crown.

Preparation is here used in the sense of doing something to become an instrument or a receptive vessel. The choice of Keter as the objective is based on its superiority to all the other Sefirot, and the fact that there is no possibility for hostile forces to enter there. Every Sefirah has its own essence, which becomes the very factor that invites the opposite side. Only something that has no sides, no defined character, can be free of this danger. As has been explained about Abraham and Isaac, the chief attribute of each leaves room for failings and weaknesses, even unto a great fall.

Thus in contrast to the precise lists of Christian virtues and vices, the Jewish tradition does not define attributes as being one thing or another. Even the attribute of Chesed, for example, which is the source of love, has to be adjudged as to whether it comes from the holy or the unholy. The same thing is true of fear of God, Gevurah. Everything depends on how it is used. There is an old saying, attributed to Rabbi Simcha Bunim of Pshische, to the effect that a Jew should be good, God-fearing, and wise; but since a merely good man is liable to be lustful, a merely God-fearing man becomes a priest, and he who is only wise is open to heresy, a Jew has to be all of them together.

This way of seeing things as a whole is important in many ways, in the inner as well as the external life. That which can be very admirable at first may end up by becoming its opposite. Out of Abraham came Ishmael, out of Isaac came Esau. Jacob's descendants seem to have managed to end up on the side of the holy, but this was so precisely because Abraham and Isaac personified extremes in terms of the Sefirot—Chesed and Gevurah—whereas Jacob personified the merging of the two in the Sefirah of Tiferet, an Attribute of harmony and beauty, free of the evils of extremism. But in the Attribute of Keter, the demonic forces have absolutely no foothold.

Another factor in the unique circumstance of receiving the Torah is the Wilderness. Wilderness is a sign of human neglect and abandon, of land that belongs to no one and has no landmarks that prohibit trespassing. One can go anywhere, in any direction. In order to receive the Torah, one has to relinquish identity and purpose (which belong to the cultivated land) and be nullified before God. Only in the highest Sefirah of Keter is such an abandonment possible.

This is another reason for the repeated saying, "I am the Lord your God who took you out of the land of Egypt (Mitzraim)." The word Mitzraim consists of the syllables "maitzar" to make narrow and "yam" (מיצר–ים). "Yam" means sea and is the symbol for Malchut (the last Sefirah, Kingdom). But Malchut is also representative of the whole of the earth, including the seas. Indeed Malchut has many different names, such as Shechinah, Jerusalem, the diamond, and the Sea; it is said that it has seventy faces, each with its own facet of being. Each has its own way of being infinitely receptive (for instance, the diamond absorbs and reflects all the colors; the sea, all the waters). As the earth, Malchut receives all the seeds of life and engenders growth; as the sea, it is even more basically receptive, with all reality emptying itself into it. The withdrawal action of Malchut becomes the Maitzar-yam, the contraction (maitzar) of the infinite sea to enable the worlds of Creation, Formation, and Action to come into existence. The highest world of Emanation (Atzilut) also descends but it hides itself in the lower worlds, and it is so well concealed that, as it is written in the Book of Proverbs, "its feet go down to death." The esoteric meaning is that it descends to bring to life the seventy rulers of the nations (which corresponds also to the seventy faces

293

of Malchut); they are the "other" gods who receive their divinity from behind. An understanding of this requires deeper knowledge of the esoteric, of course, but even in conventional language the word "other" ("Acher" in Hebrew) has connotations of rejection, unlike the neutral word "different." Thus the phrase "other gods" has derogatory meaning, implying that they receive the Divine Name from unholy sources, that they come from behind, so to speak.

Certain writings speak of the 120 different forms of the Divine Name in all the possible combinations of letters and vowels. Of these, seventy-two are of a holy order while forty-eight are of an unholy order. The demonic forces receive much of their power from this other side of divinity. Altogether the matter of Divine Name is related to Gevurah, severity and constriction (because by giving something a name, one is defining and "restricting" it). It therefore leaves room for Divine concealment on many levels. What do these other gods do?

Actually the other gods have much of the aspect of the shells or the "separated out." Anything that belongs to the holy knows with what it identifies and where it has to be, whereas the shell, in spite of once having had something of the Divine in it, is now estranged from reality and belongs to nothing at all. That is what makes it a shell, something to be discarded. The otherness makes for the existence of a shell. As a result of the concealment of the Divine, there is room for the formation of many levels of shell, many combinations of the Divine Name whose "feet are going down to death," because this descent of Malchut to death to resuscitate the world, brings life to everything, the good and the bad. As an allegory, we may take the irrigation of a citrus grove in the dry season, with the water gushing to every tree and at the same time bringing to life all the other plants and troublesome growths that had been weeded out with such difficulty. Once the valve is opened, it is impossible to control the life-giving power of the water, but if there is no water at all the fruit trees as well as the weed plants would all perish. In the same way, the descent of Malchut to the earth influences all reality, nourishing all the forms of creation.

One of the passages in the midnight prayer, Tikun Chatzot, refers to the Gentiles coming to your (God's) place "and being nourished thereby." Anyone who comes into His domain is fed and sustained. As the Psalmist reminds us: ערו ערו עד היסוד בה, "Destroy, destroy it, unto the very foundations thereof" (Psalms 137:7). "Happy is he who shall repay thee thy recompense for what thou hast done to us" (Psalm 137:7,8) hints at a complex Kabbalistic design by which the unclean, even unto its foundations, receives force by way of the forty-eight gates of pollution. Egypt, as the "narrow sea" of the Upper World, contracts to become the Egypt below, with its narrowness so expanded as to be able to absorb the holiness and let it get choked. Joseph is the example given.

This notion is perhaps the reason for the Talmudic dispute with the citizens of Jericho who recited a different version of the "Shema" prayer, and the Sages did not interfere. What were they doing? They simply made their main declaration of "Hear O Israel, the Lord is our God, the Lord is One" and followed it immediately with "And thou shalt

295

love the Lord thy God with all thy heart and all thy soul and all thy might." They did not say "Blessed is the Name, the glory of His kingdom forever and ever" in between the two, as is customary for all of Israel.

They did not want to say "Blessed is the Name" because that would introduce Malchut, the Kingdom, which had the power to raise other gods. It is explained elsewhere that the Shema prayer declaration is itself quite complete; there is nothing to add, it is itself the highest unity. The trouble is that this unity, this declaration of aspiration to Divine Unity, is a negation of all reality. It says that there is nothing else besides Him, and in this respect the world is abrogated, nothing is left of reality because there is nothing but God. But since we do have to come back to the world somehow, the ancients introduced the statement, "Blessed is the Name, the glory of His Kingdom forever," because we need the Divine Kingdom, Malchut, which emphasizes His presence below and gives life to all that exists. Thus reality is restored and we can get down from the great heights of the sublime unity and relate to God with our love.

There is a profound Kabbalistic meaning, then, in inserting the name of the glory of His Kingdom forever between the two Bible verses of the Shema declaration. It is a grasp of the reality of the world from a very clear and firm perspective. It is an endeavor to raise it from within, to lift this lower reality by virtue of the name of His Kingdom which is eternity. Whereas the Shema declaration of Divine Unity nullifies reality and the self, the blessing of the name of His Kingdom ברוך שם כבוד מלכותו לעולם ועד, in spite of its extolling the Divine, is also an acceptance of the world as it is. Incidentally, at least in the esoteric tradition, the reason this statement is uttered in a whisper is that it is a dangerous declaration that validates the reality of this world as it is given to us. We are ashamed to pledge ourselves to accept it precisely as it is – including breakfast and the evils of society, including beauty and goodness and terror. It is uttered aloud only on Yom Kippur, the Day of Atonement, when we do not eat breakfast, when we feel that we have been purified sufficiently to be able to declare openly that reality is positive. But the people of Jericho used to conjoin the two Shema declarations because they dreaded introducing this matter of Malchut, the indiscriminate power of the Divine in the present. They preferred to nullify themselves in sublimity and not allow for the rising up of any other kind of reality. They did not want to make contact with the "other" side of things, other gods, engendered by the blessing of the Name. And this is indeed a question that one has the right to pose.

The concept of Mitzraim, the narrow place of restriction and constraint below, has its parallel above. Indeed the confining reality on earth is only an expression of some limiting restraining power in the higher spheres, for nothing can manifest in reality unless it comes from a higher level. In fact, all raising up of that which has fallen and all restitution of wrong have to admit that evil has its root above, that its origin is in the wholeness. All that seems to be so corrupt here below comes from some root design that can assume any number of faces. So the Exodus from Mitzraim, is, in esoteric terms of Malchut, an emerging from the restriction of the Lower Worlds – Briyah, Yetzirah, and Assiyah. It is

the rising up of Knesset Yisrael from the human confine-
ments of Mitzraim and a bursting out into another dimension. As it is written: "Who is it that comes forth from the
wilderness" (Song of Songs 3:6); it is an emergence from the
"wilderness" state. As is the nature of the breaking out of
Malchut, the rising up is in two stages at once. One is that
exemplified by the counting of the Omer; it is a work of
steady climbing, higher and higher, and it involves repairing
detailed wrongness in thought and deed as well as conscious
pulling of oneself out of the morass of Malchut, the
Kingdom of the world. The second stage is an enlightenment, sudden and complete, in the aspect of Keter. Corresponding to the holiday of Shavuot (Pentecost), it is the total
reception of the Light of the Torah. And since the Sefirah of
Keter dominates, there is no room for the lower forces and
demonic powers to enter. These two ways of getting out of
the "narrow place"—the rising by a climbing effort and the
emergence that happens when great light illumines—have
to take their own time and their own course beyond time,
and they are also in certain ways simultaneous. At the same
time that one is trying to rise, one can be illumined or
enlightened from "within." A person may be troubled by a
temptation or a sin and manage to conquer it, but the
temptation is still there; it has not really been overcome,
only defeated in a specific confrontation. On the other hand,
sometimes one gets rid of a temptation for good, so it ceases
to trouble one endlessly. This is of the power of the light
that comes as a gift from on high. And it is a very tangible
experience; all men have known it. Even children are constantly overcoming their evil impulses. How easy it is to see

the effect of the light on a child for whom a coveted trifle suddenly becomes irrelevant. Even a Tzadik in his so-called holy perfection is no more than a man for whom most of the ordinary human desires have become irrelevant. He finds it hard to imagine an evil impulse. The point is that the antagonist has to be entirely uprooted and not simply left behind. That really is the meaning of the phrase, "For I am the One who took you out of the Land of Mitzraim."

Here too, the אנוכי (Anochi) or "I" is of the order of the Sefirah of Keter (every name of God relates to a certain Sefirah). It is only by the great power of Keter that Mitzraim, the land of double narrowness, the place of constriction and human corruption, can be overcome. The Anochi who takes us out of Egypt is of great significance, and the Kabbalistic interpretation is very profound and complex. After all, there is a dynamic relationship between Keter and Malchut, and another sort of relationship exists between Malchut and Galut Mitzraim, the Egyptian Exile.

The concept of the Egyptian Exile, the state of being at the lowest layer of corruption, has many aspects, both national historical and personal individual. Every breaking forth into freedom is a being taken out of Egypt. We may note too that not at every stage is this Egyptian Exile unpleasant. At the time of Joseph it was more than a haven, and for a long time it was a source of wealth and power for the children of Israel. Only later did it become unbearable, a state of enslavement. The analogy may extend to a universal scale.

On a purely personal level, it seems that we go through a similar process every day. We are forever descending to the reality of the world, and often the situation is comfortable and we get used to it. But it soon develops into the narrow place of restriction and bondage, and so we cry out in prayer, "Shema Yisrael" to help us get out.

On the cosmic plane, too, the Egyptian Exile is a name for the loss of Divine Light in the Klipah or Shell. "Other" gods take over. True, God goes down with us to Egypt as well, but the Keter of Anochi, the I who takes you out of Egypt, is the key to human freedom. It is a permanent promise as well as a historical statement, and that is the primordial essence of Keter. It is not the I who created the heaven and the earth, it is the I who took you out of Egypt. This "I" is also concerned about us; he came to remain close by virtue of Torah. The Creator of heaven and earth is paradoxically not the same one as the giver of the Torah. And Torah is the possibility for man to be liberated forever from bondage to heaven and earth.

For there is on one hand the bondage of the reality of the world and the gap between heaven and earth, and there is also the I, the Lord your God, who explains that He is the one who took you out of bondage – out of the narrow places of the earth and the enslavement to all physicality. And this again is the introduction to the Torah, which then assumes its greater meaning: that Torah is a release from death itself. It is the freedom from all bondage, the ultimate liberation.

About the Author

Rabbi Adin Steinsaltz is internationally regarded as one of the leading rabbis of this century. The author of many books, he is best known for his monumental translation of and commentary on the Talmud.

About the Translator

Yehuda Hanegbi is a writter, editor, playwright, and translator living in Jerusalem.